# TIME
## FOR KIDS
### EXPLORERS

# ROBOTS

By Mark Shulman
and
James Buckley Jr.

NASA

SIM

HONDA

POLICE

**TIME FOR KIDS**
**Editor** Nellie Gonzalez Cutler
**Creative Director** Jennifer Kraemer-Smith
**Project Editor** Brenda Iasevoli

*TIME HOME ENTERTAINMENT*
**Publisher** Jim Childs
**Vice President, Brand & Digital Strategy** Steven Sandonato
**Executive Director, Marketing Services** Carol Pittard
**Executive Director, Retail & Special Sales** Tom Mifsud
**Executive Publishing Director** Joy Bomba
**Director, Bookazine Development & Marketing** Laura Adam
**Vice President, Finance** Vandana Patel
**Publishing Director** Megan Pearlman
**Assistant General Counsel** Simone Procas
**Assistant Director, Special Sales** Ilene Schreider
**Brand Manager** Jonathan White
**Associate Prepress Manager** Alex Voznesenskiy
**Associate Production Manager** Kimberly Marshall
**Associate Project Manager** Stephanie Braga
**Cover Design By** Beth Bugler

**Editorial Director** Stephen Koepp
**Senior Editor** Roe D'Angelo
**Copy Chief** Rina Bander
**Design Manager** Anne-Michelle Gallero
**Editorial Operations** Gina Scauzillo

**Created at Oomf, Inc.**
www.Oomf.com

**By** Mark Shulman and James Buckley Jr.
**Designed By** Bill Madrid
**Educational Consultant** Kara Pranikoff

**Special thanks:** Katherine Barnet, Brad Beatson, Jeremy Biloon, Conor Buckley, Susan Chodakiewicz, Rose Cirrincione, Dos Pueblos Engineering Academy staff, Robert Englander, Assu Etsubneh, Mariana Evans, Christine Font, Susan Hettleman, Hillary Hirsch, David Kahn, Jean Kennedy, Hazlitt Krog, Amy Mangus, Nina Mistry, Dave Rozzelle, Ricardo Santiago, Holly Smith, Craig Sparer, Adriana Tierno

For information on TIME FOR KIDS magazine for the
classroom or home, go to TIMEFORKIDS.COM
or call 1-800-777-8600.
For subscriptions to SI KIDS, go to
SIKIDS.COM or call 1-800-889-6007.

Published by TIME FOR KIDS Books,
An imprint of Time Home Entertainment Inc.
1271 Avenue of the Americas, 6th floor
New York, NY 10020

ISBN 10: 1-61893-373-6
ISBN 13: 978-1-61893-373-7
Library of Congress Control Number: 2014932410

TIME FOR KIDS is a trademark of Time Inc.

We welcome your comments and suggestions about TIME FOR KIDS Books. Please write to us at:
TIME FOR KIDS Books, Attention: Book Editors, P.O. Box 11016, Des Moines, IA 50336-1016
If you would like to order any of our hardcover Collector's Edition books, please call us at 1-800-327-6388
(Monday through Friday, 7 a.m. to 8 p.m., or Saturday, 7 a.m. to 6 p.m., Central Time).

# TIME
## FOR · KIDS
### EXPLORERS

# ROBOTS

**ROBOT** *noun* \ rō-bät \

1 a : A machine that performs complex actions, similar to humans or other animals; also, a machine that can perform repetitive tasks, guided by automatic controls.

2 a fictional machine that mimics human actions, but without emotions

# The Robots Are Coming

**N**ot very long ago, robots were a fantasy of storybooks. Fictional robots could be our perfect servants, giving us freedom to zoom in our space cars, . . . or they could take over the world with their sub-atomic pulsing laser cannons.

**In real life,** robots help build our cars and they vacuum our floors. (That's a good start.) Robots play ping-pong and basketball and soccer. (That's even better.) Robots today help doctors perform surgery, and help people walk again. (Now you're talking.) Modern robots are even sent in to fight fires, catch crooks, deal with bombs, and save lives. (Awesome!) Of course, robots can also spy on you from the sky, beat you in chess, and eventually be a whole lot smarter than you are. (Um, wait a minute.)

**The fact is,** robots are getting smarter, stronger, and more agile, and they're going to be everywhere. Inside this fascinating book, you'll get to see the latest and most interesting robots that exist today. And you'll find them in all kinds of places: in the sky, at home, in the science lab, and on the front lines. *TIME FOR KIDS Explorers: Robots* uses dazzling photos, fun facts, and a bright, electric presentation to give you the very latest on bright, electric robots.

**Robots are working** for us in many new and exciting ways. Find out what you can expect in the near future from our helpful, diligent, loyal robot servants. And here's hoping they stay that way! Because the robots aren't just coming . . .

## They're already here!

## "This book explores the incredible world of robots."

*Previous generations could only dream about these exciting machines, or maybe see them in comic books or movies. But today, real robots are everywhere. They build our cars, clean our houses, help our soldiers, and even perform medical surgery. I hope the facts in this book amaze you as much as they do me. I look at all of these beautiful, sophisticated machines and say to myself, "If this is what we can do today, who knows what we will do tomorrow?"*

*Remember, part of this book's title is "Explorers." I hope these pages will inspire you to be curious, to discover new ways of doing things, and to make your ideas a reality even if people say they can't be achieved. Robots and all of the other fantastic machines in our world are the results of people just like you who dreamed of extraordinary things and asked, "Why not?"*

**– Dean Kamen**
**Founder, FIRST Robotics**

*The FIRST Robotics Competition is an annual international high school robotics competition.*

7

# SIX DEGREES OF
# ROBOTS

Different kinds of robots do different kinds of jobs. Whatever the job, robots are built to make life easier, save lives, and may someday even look alive. Which robot for which job? Nearly all the robots we can imagine fall into one of the following six categories, ranging from human-controlled to self-controlled to robots that can think for themselves.

## Tele-robot

Humans control the movements of these robots via remote control.

Like tele-robots, these are run by remote control. But telepresence robots have cameras that communicate what the robot sees and hears to the operator.

## Telepresence

## Static

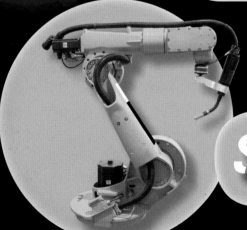

These industrial robots are the most simple independent robots. Once they're programmed, they don't need humans to operate. Static means they don't travel, but they do swing their arms around to build and handle materials.

# Mobile

Robots that can move on their own are mobile. They use preprogrammed routes or they "read" their environment and steer themselves.

# Autonomous

These can move on their own, take in energy from the environment, and change their actions to fit the task. There are very few of these advanced robots.

# Android

These are robots that are designed to look and act like humans. The photo shows a statue of actor Arnold Schwarzenegger playing an android in the movie *The Terminator*.

# Isaac Asimov's "Three Laws of Robotics"

Isaac Asimov was a popular science fiction author who wrote many stories involving robots, including *I, Robot*. In 1942, Asimov introduced his now-famous Three Laws of Robotics—the ironclad laws that iron giants must absolutely follow. The Three Laws are:

**1.** **A robot may not injure** a human being or, through inaction, allow a human being to come to harm.

**2.** **A robot must obey** the orders given to it by human beings, except where such orders would conflict with the First Law.

**3.** **A robot must protect** its own existence as long as such protection does not conflict with the First or Second Law.

# EXPLORING ROBOTS IN HISTORY

People have dreamed of making mechanical human beings for centuries. The great Italian artist Leonardo da Vinci drew up plans for a machine that looked like a knight. The novel *Frankenstein* was about a scientist making a man into a living machine. Those dreams began to come true in the 20th century. Electricity, new discoveries in materials, and the coming of computers gave scientists—and dreamers—the skills to make robots a big part of our lives today.

## 1900

### Automatic Man

This human-like machine was designed by New Yorker Louis Perew to pull a carriage. It ran on an electric battery and was one of several attempts by early designers to create machines that worked and looked like people.

### Tik-Tok of Oz

Fiction inspired the ideas of robot makers. Author L. Frank Baum introduced the roly-poly Tik-Tok character in his Oz series. Though Tik-Tok wasn't called a robot in the story, this mechanical man is considered to be the first bot to appear in literature.

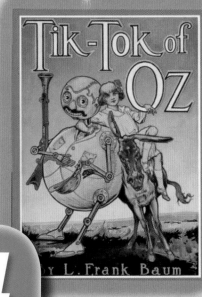

## 1914

# 1945

## First Robot

This prop from a play gave the world the word "robot." Karel Capek wrote a play called "R.U.R." Machines made by a character in the play were called "robota," which means "worker" in Capek's Czech language. The word became "robot" in English.

## Robots That Think?

Alan Turing created the idea of robots that "think." He used his genius to break Nazi codes in World War II with this Enigma machine. His ideas set the computer age in motion.

# 1948

## Rolling Robot

Grey Walter made robot "turtles" such as Elsie. They were among the first robots to use electronics and to move in response to programming.

# EXPLORING ROBOTS IN HISTORY

## 1951

### Robots on Film

The tall, silver Gort apperaed in *The Day the Earth Stood Still*. The 8-foot alien robot lands on Earth with the mission to destroy humans if they can't live peacefully. The filmmakers guessed that alien worlds would make humanoid robots first.

## 1961

### One Arm First

Unimate was the first robot "arm." It could be programmed to do the same job over and over, such as in a factory or a lab. A humanoid robot was more than a decade away.

### Astro Boy

Astro Boy began in the comics in Japan, but in 1963, he starred in what became a popular TV series. Astro Boy was made to mimic a real boy . . . but with superpowers.

## 1963

# 1966

# 1969

## Robby

The TV show *Lost in Space* featured the talkative Robby the Robot, who aided the spaceship flown by the Robinson family.

## Moving Ahead

This Stanford Arm was named for the university where it was developed. It was the first electric-powered, computer-controlled robot arm, and it signaled a leap forward in robotics.

# 1970

## Shakey

Shakey, named after the way it moved, was the first robot that could move by itself while sensing the world around it. Shakey used sensors to move on both programmed and unplanned routes. The bot was created at the Stanford Research Institute. Shakey's abilities were groundbreaking in robotics at the time.

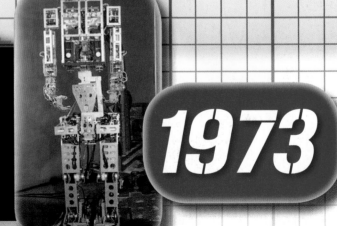

## Wabot

This robot, made at Japan's Waseda University, is considered the first real humanoid robot. The inventors were trying to figure out how to make a robot walk.

# 1973

## 1975

### Arms Race

The science of making precision robot arms continued to improve. This PUMA robot was the start of wide use of such arms on assembly lines in factories. The original is in the Smithsonian Institution.

## 1987

## 1997

### Meet Data

An android is a robot that can look and act just like a human being. On the TV show *Star Trek: The Next Generation*, Brent Spiner played Data. The character was an android Starfleet officer capable of brilliant thought—yet it wanted to feel emotions like a human.

### Sojourner

NASA landed a rover named Sojourner on Mars. The rover sent back the first images and information about the Red Planet. Sojourner's success proved that robots could do jobs that humans could not.

# 1999

## Woof!

Advances in electronics meant that robots could be smaller and smaller. Aibo was one of the first popular robot toys. Kids could program it to walk, talk, or lie down.

# 2000

## Asimo

This walking, talking robot from Japan was a breakthrough. More human-like than previous robots, it could walk up stairs, carry things, and interact with people.

# 2010

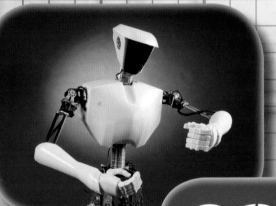

## Charli

Scientists at the University of Virginia created the first humanoid robot in the United States. Charli could walk, kick, and use its sensitive fingers to pick up objects.

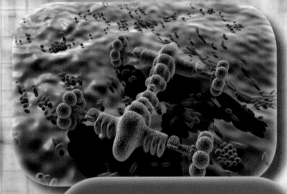

# 20??

## Next!

Scientists are turning their attention to smaller robots. Nanotechnology is making robots smaller than human cells. The next frontier of robotics is actually inside people.

# EXPLORING ROBOTS THAT WORK

Science fiction is now science fact. Thousands of robots work in factories, laboratories, and other businesses. Robots can do the same task over and over without getting tired, so they are perfect for jobs that might be dangerous, painful, or too precise for humans. When it's time to get to work, call a robot!

**19**

## Robot Arms

**18**

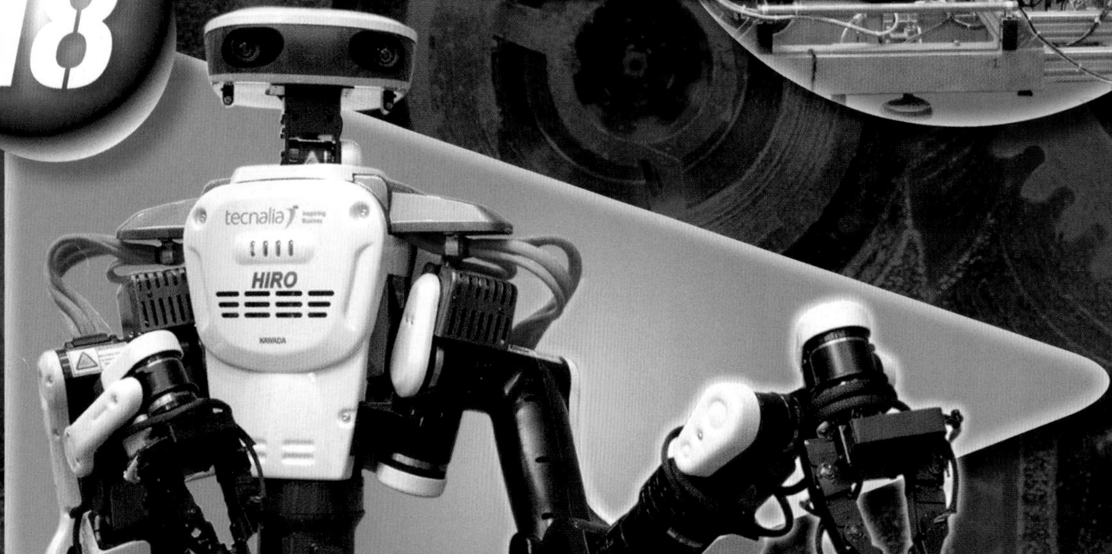

## Robot Hands

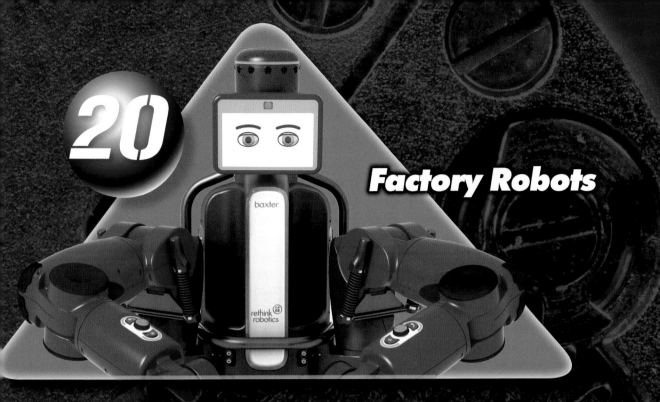

**20** Factory Robots

**Strong Robots**

**22**

**23**

Robots on the Go

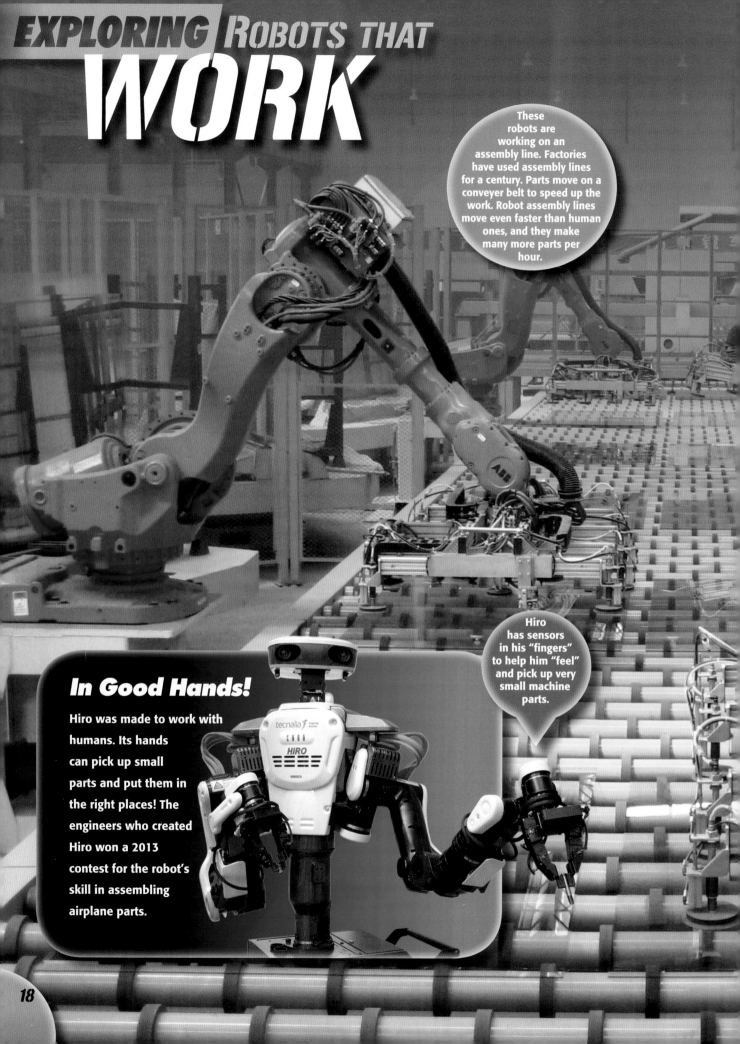

# EXPLORING ROBOTS THAT WORK

These robots are working on an assembly line. Factories have used assembly lines for a century. Parts move on a conveyer belt to speed up the work. Robot assembly lines move even faster than human ones, and they make many more parts per hour.

Hiro has sensors in his "fingers" to help him "feel" and pick up very small machine parts.

## In Good Hands!

Hiro was made to work with humans. Its hands can pick up small parts and put them in the right places! The engineers who created Hiro won a 2013 contest for the robot's skill in assembling airplane parts.

# Robots Get to Work!

Factory robots like these can do the same job over and over and never make a mistake. They are programmed to make a series of movements that help construct parts for airplanes, automobiles, computers, and much more. The robots not only do the job perfectly, they don't get tired and never need a day off!

The single-arm industrial robot is the most common type in the world. Its arm can swing in just about any direction.

ABB

# EXPLORING ROBOTS THAT WORK

A sonar dome detects nearby humans by sound.

Baxter's joints allow its arms to move in more directions than human arms. This flexibility is one advantage that robots have over human workers.

## Meet Baxter the Bot

Industrial robots are getting better. The first such bots were simple arms that tackled one task over and over. Engineers knew they could top that. The result is Baxter, from Rethink Robotics. Using multiple sensors, Baxter can "see" people around him. Baxter doesn't require a technician to program it. Anyone can train this bot to do a job. If you want Baxter to pick up an object, simply take the robot's arm and guide it through the movements. Baxter stands about six feet tall with his rolling base and weighs about 300 pounds.

Baxter can have different "hands" attached for each task.

Baxter can roll or can be locked into one place.

Baxter is skilled at sorting parts. Here he is taking finished machine parts from the line and putting them in boxes.

Baxter's screen/face helps him keep an "eye" on things as he packs parts for shipping.

The tubes carry compressed air to help the robot "fingers" work.

Suction cups pick up the parcels.

# Flexible Fingers

Robot arms need different fingers for different jobs. Human operators can swap out the hands and fingers at the end of a bot's arm. Instead of fingers, this robot has suction cups to pick up boxes and lay them on a growing stack behind itself.

# EXPLORING ROBOTS THAT WORK

When robots work near people, safety is a big issue. The robots must be able to navigate around objects and people. Like other robots, REEM uses cameras in its "eyes" along with other sensors to "read" the world around it.

## The Office Robot

Imagine someday sitting at your desk in an office and a robot roams in to deliver your mail. With robots like REEM, that's not a dream, it's reality. REEM can be programmed to deliver packages and other items in an office. Cameras and sensors help it navigate without crashing into desks or people. A screen on its chest can display information, give messages or directions, or play videos. REEM roams airports and malls, guiding people to their destinations and providing them with useful information, including weather and flight times. Its screen works in many languages, too. REEM is made by Pal-Robotics of Spain.

REEM's hands can change position to carry, hold, or grasp objects.

The heavy-duty plastic "skirt" covers the wheels that let REEM go where it needs to go.

22

## Hammer Time!

Industrial robots make the workplace safer for humans. This remote-controlled jackhammer allows the worker to operate the digging tool at a safe distance.

An operator uses joy sticks to direct this robot's moves.

Some construction robots can be programmed to perform tasks solo as well.

At this factory in Germany, robot arms have helped create more than 5 million solar panels in the past decade. Using robots means faster, more efficient production. They almost never make mistakes!

The black hoses hold hydraulic fluid that helps the robot arm move.

## A Gentle Touch

A heavy-duty metal robot can be gentle. That's because engineers can program the amount of force a robot's arm uses. So robots can pick up a very delicate object like this solar panel without breaking it. Factory robots need strength, but they need to be careful, too!

23

# EXPLORING ROBOTS THAT PROTECT

Police, fire, and military personnel are deploying robots to save the day. Smart machines of all shapes and sizes are on patrol, in the streets, on the battlefields, and in many other dangerous situations. They aren't robo-cops yet, but these high-tech helpers are making a big difference in the world.

**27** Robot Police

**Rescue Robots** **29**

**28** Robot Firefighters

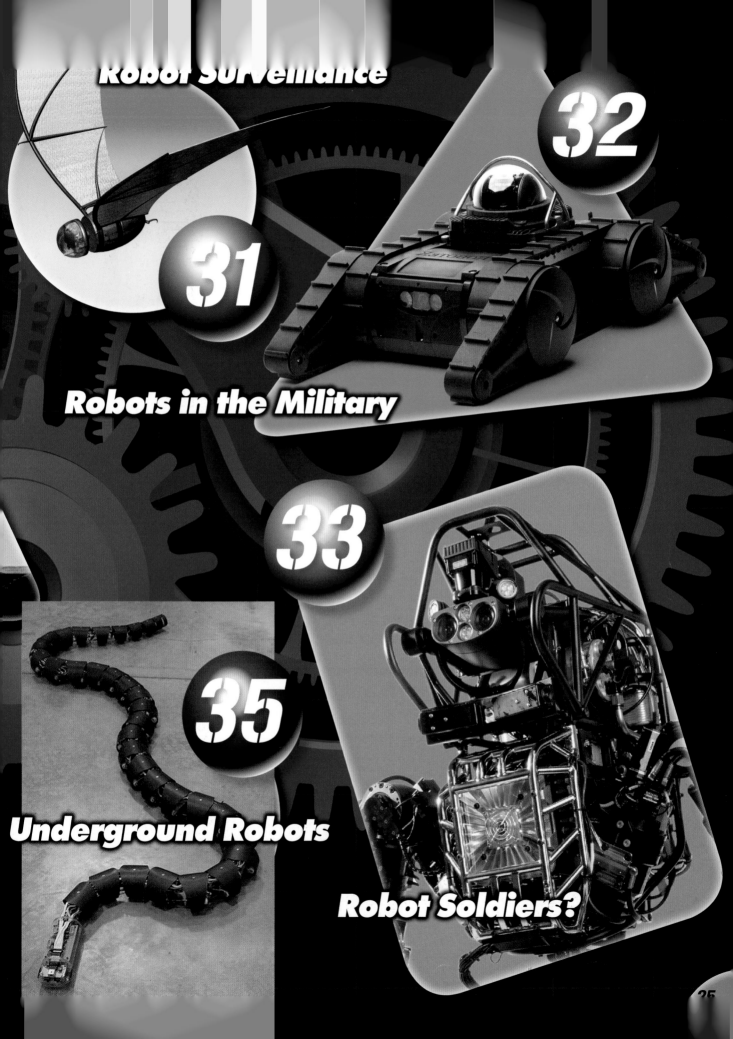

Robot Surveillance

31

32

**Robots in the Military**

33

35

**Underground Robots**

**Robot Soldiers?**

25

# PROTECT

## The Throwbot

The police often dive right into dangerous situations. It's part of their job. Throwbot gives them an advantage. Instead of rushing into a room, they can toss this bot in first. Its cameras send back pictures to the police waiting safely outside. This way police can see what they're getting into.

No matter which way Throwbot lands, its cameras and antenna will be able to beam out pictures.

# Police on Wheels

Meet Robo Sally, a rolling robot with amazing hands, from Johns Hopkins University.

Cameras can monitor public areas and keep people safe.

Strong fingers can clear away debris.

Cameras in the eyes let operators see what Sally sees.

A robot traffic stop? Robo Sally makes it easy!

## RoboCop

The idea behind Florida International University's RoboCop program is to put disabled police officers and military veterans back to work. Trained officers can control the robot from a remote location. Someday it might patrol your street!

The metal shell might be replaced with lightweight plastic.

The teleoperator would drive this robot around on its wheels.

27

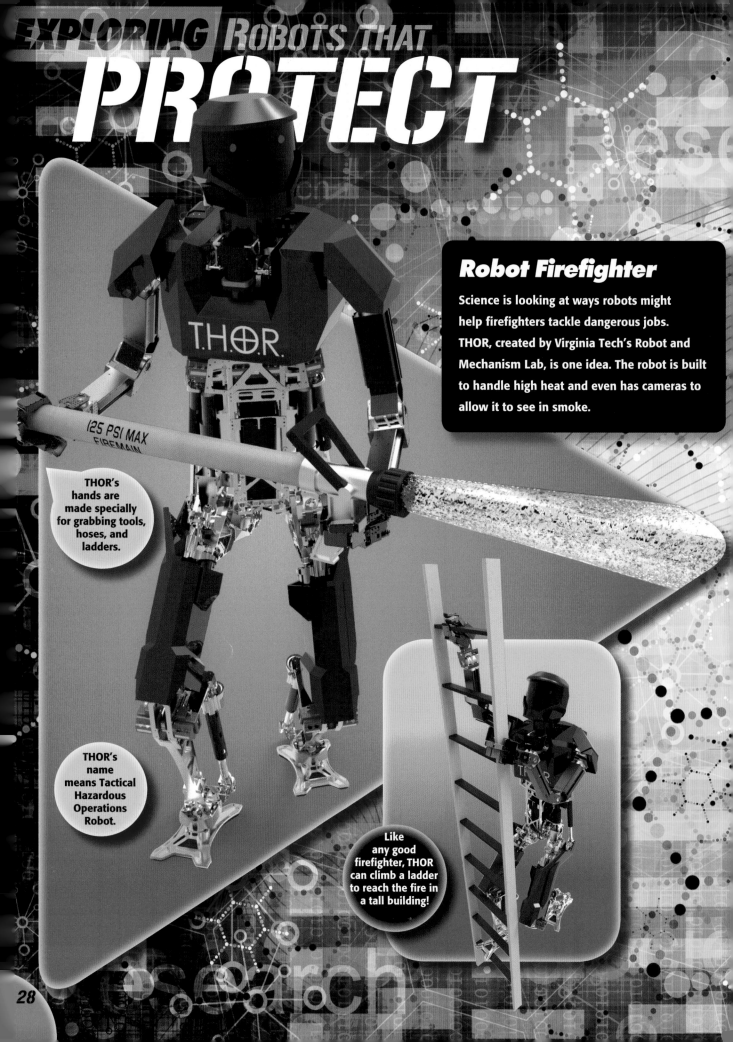

T.H.O.R.

125 PSI MAX
FIREMAIN

## Robot Firefighter

Science is looking at ways robots might help firefighters tackle dangerous jobs. THOR, created by Virginia Tech's Robot and Mechanism Lab, is one idea. The robot is built to handle high heat and even has cameras to allow it to see in smoke.

THOR's hands are made specially for grabbing tools, hoses, and ladders.

THOR's name means Tactical Hazardous Operations Robot.

Like any good firefighter, THOR can climb a ladder to reach the fire in a tall building!

## Water on the Way!

Students at Penn State helped develop this remote-controlled robot. It can be connected to a hose and then sent into a burning building. Firefighters outside safely aim the hose.

**Tracks help the robot move over rough ground.**

## Ship Fires

Fighting fires on ships creates new problems: rough seas, saltwater, dense smoke. SAFFIR, from Virginia Tech, can use water, extinguishers, and foam, and might help sailors fight fires more safely.

**Special sensors help SAFFIR balance in sea conditions.**

**This firefighter is lowering a VGTV robot into a deep hole to give him a picture of potential dangers. Then he can make the rescue.**

## Rolling Camera

In collapsed buildings or tiny spaces, firefighters need "eyes." This VGTV robot can fit into small spaces or even underwater (below) and beam back lifesaving pictures.

# PROTECT

For several years, the U.S. military has looked at ways robots can help soldiers do their jobs more safely. Robots—Ten-hut!

Turret with camera and rangefinder.

Grenade launching pods.

Heavy duty tires let the robot dig through any terrain.

## G.I. Robot

Armies of the future will be able to send robots to help them on the battlefield. The Gladiator is one example of a multi-talented, rolling arsenal. Directed by a soldier, the Gladiator can roll, shoot film, and even launch grenades.

## Safety First

This robot, called BEAR, shows a key use of robots by the military: Handling bombs or other unexploded devices.

U.S. soldiers in Iraq and Afghanistan use robots to discover devices before they can harm the soldiers.

into the bat's "head."

## Spy Bat

Look! Up in the sky! It's a bat! Wait, no . . . it's a robot! The machine, called a COM-BAT, is still being developed by the University of Michigan. The aim is to fly the bot above battlefields and send back pictures to soldiers.

Heavy duty shock absorbers let BigDog move over any terrain.

BigDog can carry a big load: More than 300 pounds of gear!

## BigDog on the Move!

Engineers looked at how animals move to design BigDog, a four-legged robot that travels with soldiers as a kind of pack animal. BigDog can run, walk, climb hills, and carry big loads. An operator controls Big Dog with a smartpad on his wrist.

# EXPLORING ROBOTS THAT PROTECT

## Safe Soldiers

Robots like First Look (shown in the inset and being thrown here) help keep soldiers safe. These little bots are rugged, durable, and flexible. They can be thrown into a room or a building and always land safely. An operator can help the robot flip right side up, move around, and take pictures. Soldiers can then decide their next move.

## On the Move

Petman can walk for days. Researchers use this robot to discover how long soldiers' uniforms will last.

Petman walks on a treadmill like a soldier on a long march.

First Look has tracks that help it move in any direction.

Double "flipper" tracks let Warrior climb over low obstacles.

## Multitask

The main job of the Warrior from iRobot is to examine and remove bombs. The operator directs Warrior to the bomb and then the powerful arm can pick it up. Cameras give experts a look at the bomb, too. Warrior can also help clean up after a disaster, search for victims in rubble, and carry dangerous chemicals or other materials.

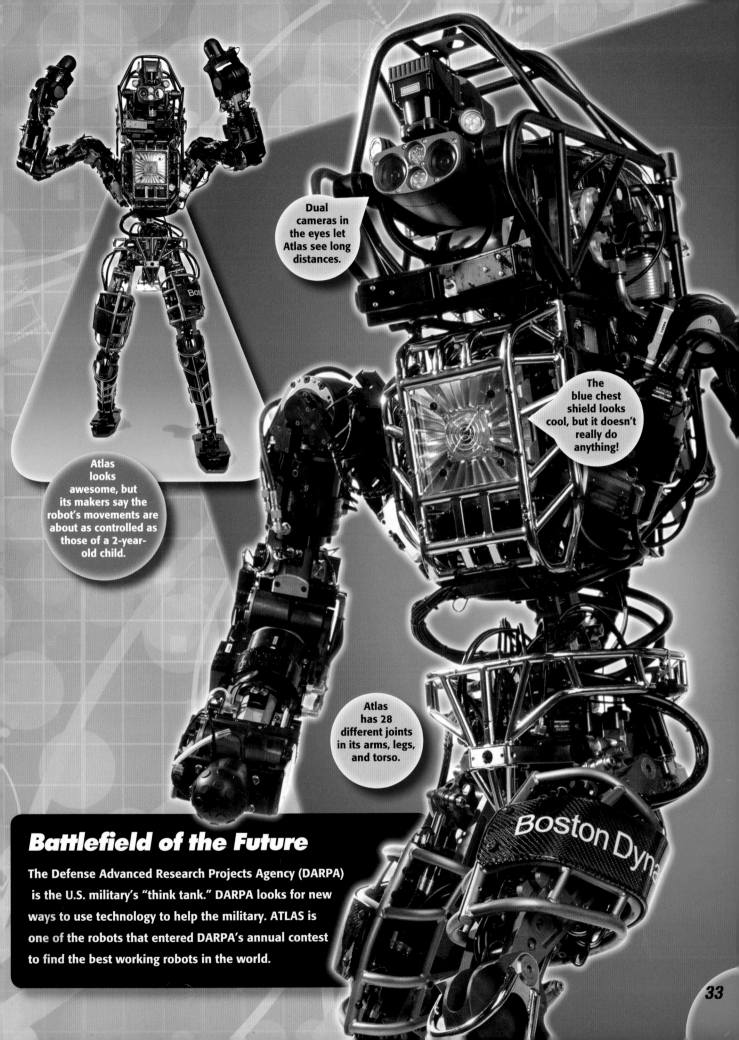

Dual cameras in the eyes let Atlas see long distances.

The blue chest shield looks cool, but it doesn't really do anything!

Atlas looks awesome, but its makers say the robot's movements are about as controlled as those of a 2-year-old child.

Atlas has 28 different joints in its arms, legs, and torso.

## Battlefield of the Future

The Defense Advanced Research Projects Agency (DARPA) is the U.S. military's "think tank." DARPA looks for new ways to use technology to help the military. ATLAS is one of the robots that entered DARPA's annual contest to find the best working robots in the world.

# EXPLORING *Robots that* PROTECT

## Tunnel Bot!

A variety of robots such as this Versatrax 150 run on tracks and carry cameras into tunnels, pipelines, and other small places. These robots go where humans cannot to stop disasters before they happen.

The metal jaws of the Power Hawk can rip open a stuck car door.

See how the tracks of these search bots change to move over flat or inclined ground.

## Rescue Tools

Rescue workers often use the "jaws of life" tool to rip open metal doors and rescue people trapped inside. This NERAT PowerHawk combines mobile robot tech with the strength of the "jaws." Rescuers can send this life-saving tool to places they couldn't reach before.

When disaster strikes, robots get to work. Around the world, robots of many kinds are used to help save people and clean up after disasters.

BEAR can lift more than 500 pounds at once!

## A Mighty BEAR

The rolling robot named BEAR can pick up bombs (page 31), but it is used more often in disaster recovery operations. BEAR is stronger than a human and never tires. It can also work in unstable buildings that might not be safe for people to enter.

## Pile Power

In a disaster, getting to trapped people quickly is vital. Robots like these can crawl safely over debris. Cameras and microphones on board help rescuers find people to save.

Like a real snake, this bot has numerous segments.

## Snake to the Rescue!

What if a space is too small for big bots to explore? Send in this snake-like robot developed in Japan. It can push through debris and investigate places no human rescuer can reach.

# EXPLORE

Along with humans or on their own, robots explore our world and beyond. Each robot has an ability to withstand extreme environments. This allows us to push the boundaries of exploration further. Robots boldly go where no one has gone before . . . from the depths of the ocean to the vastness of space.

**40**

**Robonaut**

**38**

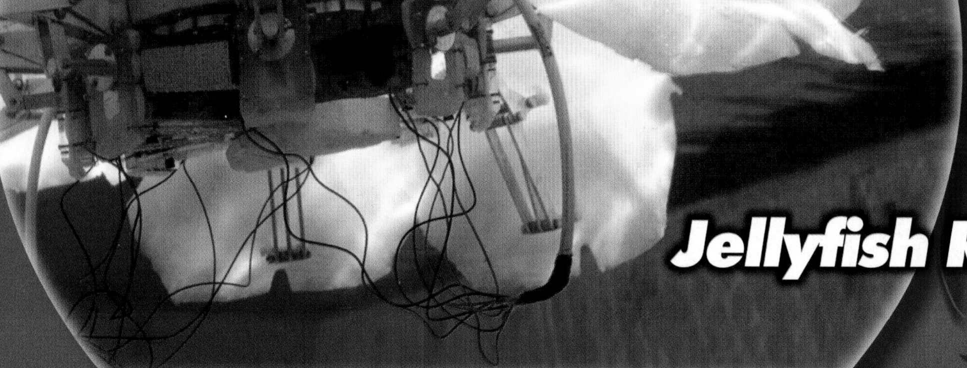

**Jellyfish Robot**

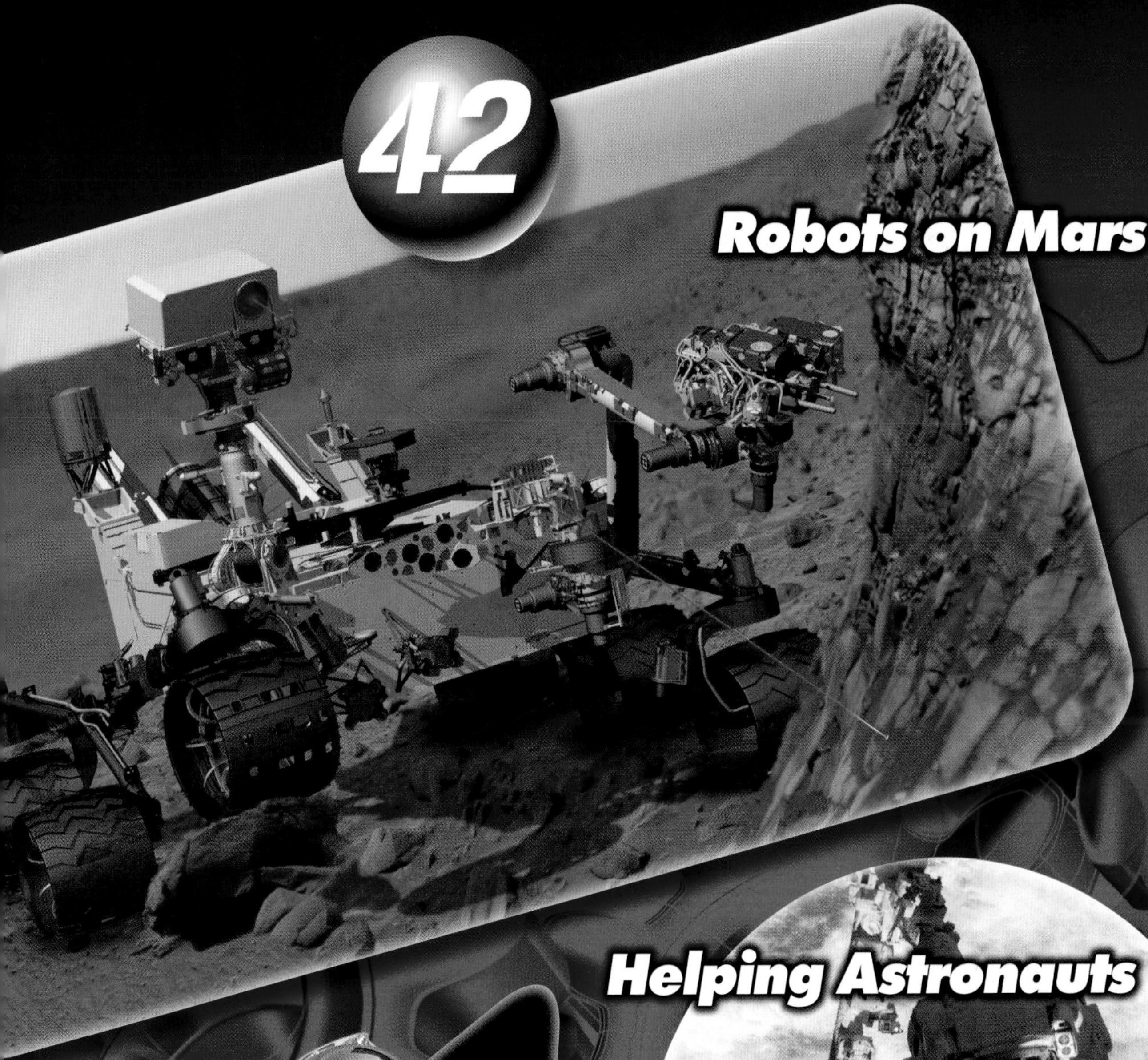



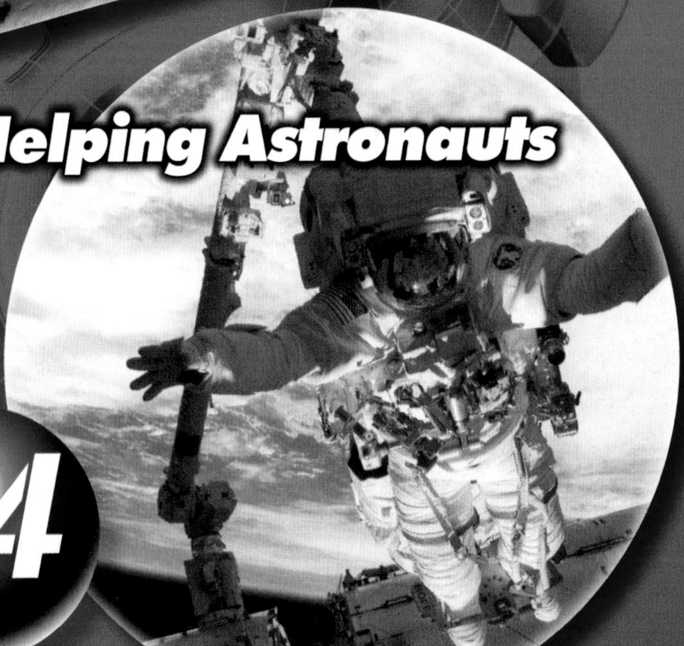

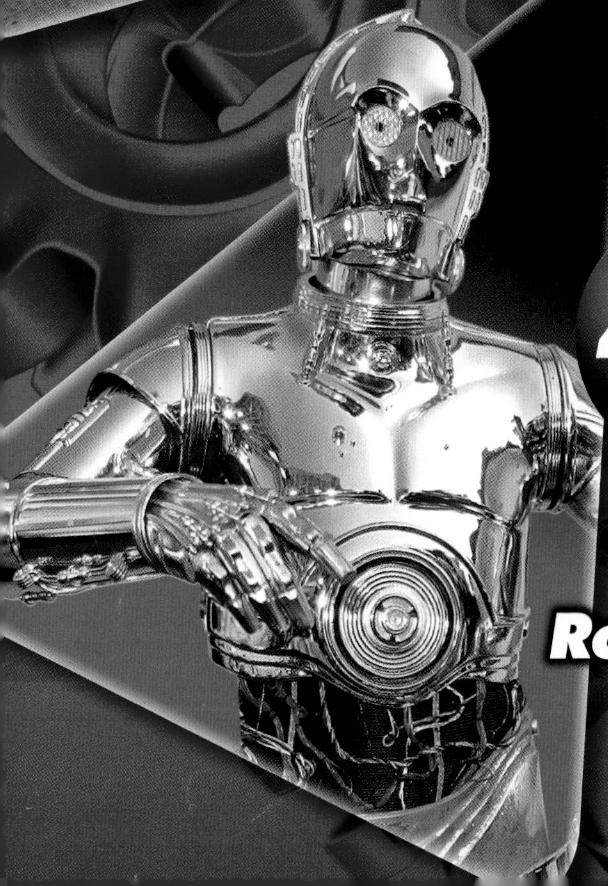

Robots make great ocean explorers. They can stay underwater longer than human divers. Plus, robots can be built to handle life in the deep sea, frigid temperatures and all. Just think: The next sea creature you see may be keeping an eye on our oceans.

A metal sensor panel on top of Cyro helps it communicate with controllers.

## A Jelly Bot?

Meet Cyro, a 6-foot wide, 170-pound jellyfish robot. Cyro gets its name from a large jellyfish species called *Cyanea capillata*, plus the word robot. Its rubbery body drifts with the current, much as a jellyfish does. Its giant size can hold enough power to stay in the ocean for months. Students from Virginia Tech created Cyro with funding from the U.S. Navy. The bot may someday act as an undersea spy for the military, monitor oil spills, or make detailed maps of the ocean floor.

## MegaDeep

Exploring the deepest parts of the ocean can be dangerous for humans, but not for robots. DEPTHX was created with help from NASA. Piloted from the surface, this robot can dive into the deepest caverns of the ocean floor. Its cameras and other instruments bring back information about this often-mysterious part of our planet.

Bright spotlights allow for filming in the dark ocean.

Arms fold up into DEPTHX while it dives; they can extend when it reaches its destination.

## Go, Fish, Go!

The Slocum glider was named for Josiah Slocum, the first man to sail solo around the world. The glider can swim for days at a time on a programmed course. It beams back information that helps scientists study ocean currents, temperature, and more.

## Who Needs a Captain?

College students from Rhode Island set out to build the first unmanned boat to cross the Atlantic Ocean. About three years, five models, and thousands of dollars later, they did it. The team launched the solar-powered Scout from Sakonnet Point, Rhode Island, and fans tracked the boat's progress online. After more than 1,300 miles, something went wrong. Online tracking showed Scout was drifting. Still, the project enjoyed some success. Scout claimed the record for longest voyage by an unmanned boat.

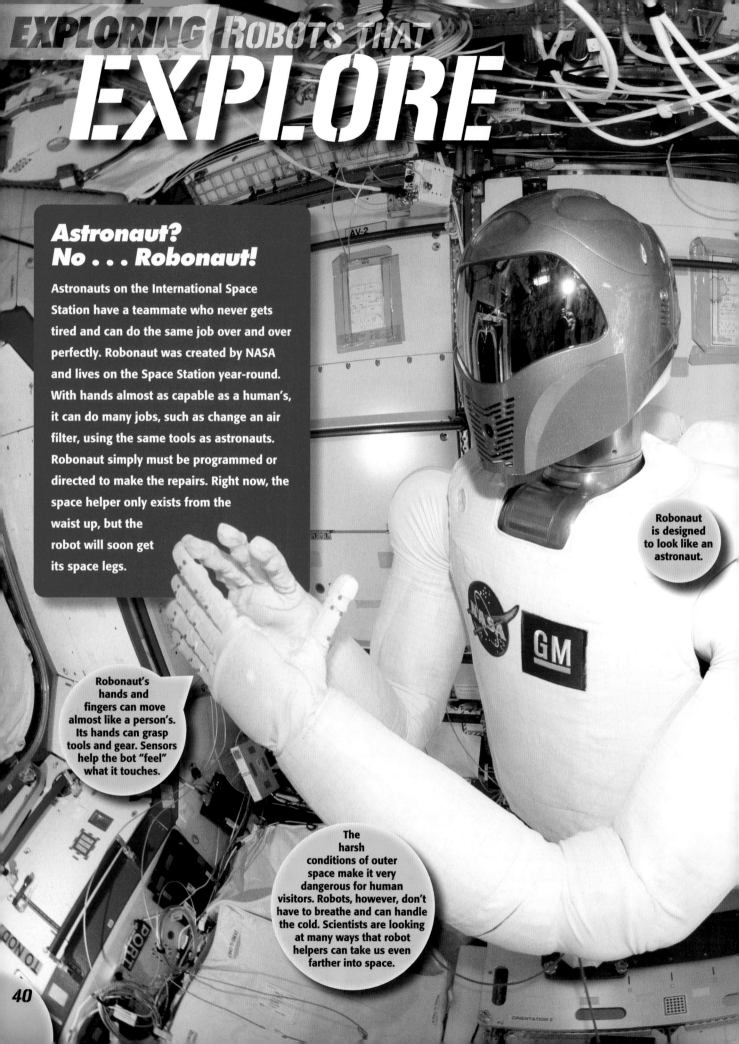

# EXPLORING ROBOTS THAT EXPLORE

## Astronaut? No . . . Robonaut!

Astronauts on the International Space Station have a teammate who never gets tired and can do the same job over and over perfectly. Robonaut was created by NASA and lives on the Space Station year-round. With hands almost as capable as a human's, it can do many jobs, such as change an air filter, using the same tools as astronauts. Robonaut simply must be programmed or directed to make the repairs. Right now, the space helper only exists from the waist up, but the robot will soon get its space legs.

Robonaut is designed to look like an astronaut.

Robonaut's hands and fingers can move almost like a person's. Its hands can grasp tools and gear. Sensors help the bot "feel" what it touches.

The harsh conditions of outer space make it very dangerous for human visitors. Robots, however, don't have to breathe and can handle the cold. Scientists are looking at many ways that robot helpers can take us even farther into space.

Robonaut can't send a text message—yet!

Here's Robonaut without some of his clothing. This shows his heavy-duty metal arms and the many joints of the fingers.

NASA is looking at craft such as this Centaur to let Robonaut explore other worlds.

Humans can't visit other planets (yet!) but robots can. Some of the most advanced robots have helped explore Mars.

## Desert Bot

Zoe roams Chile's Atacama Desert testing instruments for future Mars missions. The rover digs for soil samples. Scientists say underground is the best place to search for life on Mars.

An onboard "lab" can test samples and send the results to NASA.

Metal wheels dig into the soft soil on Mars.

## Roaming Around Mars

As you read this, NASA's Curiosity robot rover is moving across the Martian landscape. Packed with instruments, Curiosity is making new discoveries all the time and sending the news to Earth.

## Testing 1, 2

Curiosity is the latest in a line of successful Mars rovers that started with Sojourner in 1997. In the photo, NASA scientists wear "clean suits" as they work on an early version of Curiosity. Dust or dirt could harm the delicate instruments used to build the rover.

Arms extend to drill or pick up samples.

Laser beams hit the rocks and Curiosity tests the dust that flies off.

## Wheels in Motion

Curiosity travels about 660 feet each day on six wheels, each with individual motors. The wheels' metal rims and flexible joints help the rover take on tough terrain and to turn in a complete circle.

# EXPLORE

From rovers to robonauts to giant mechanical arms, robotic technology has played a big part in space exploration. Robots can go where humans cannot. Plus, they can take on tedious tasks, leaving scientists more time for space research.

## What a Trip!

No robot has traveled farther than Voyager. This NASA space probe was launched in 1977 and has explored Jupiter, Saturn, Uranus, and Neptune. In 2013, it became the first manmade object to leave the solar system. It is now about 12 billion miles from our sun.

The white dish is an antenna that beams information back to Earth.

This astronaut is being moved into position at the end of the robot arm called Dextre.

This long arm measures magnetic waves.

Fluent in more than six million forms of communication.

The robot arm also can deploy satellites.

## Robots from Far, Far Away

Science fiction loves robots, too! Books, movies, and TV shows have used robots in space stories for decades. Two of the most famous fictional robots are R2-D2 (on left) and C3PO (on right) from the Star Wars series. R2 interacted with machines, but C3PO could communicate with both humans and machines. Though often frustrated by R2's antics, C3PO still worked with the tiny 'bot to save the galaxy.

Not.

**One of Dextre's jobs was to move cargo from the shuttle to the station.**

## *Super Dextre!*

Created by Canadian scientists, Dextre is the multi-armed robotic "handyman" attached to the International Space Station. Dextre can replace outside parts such as batteries and cameras, move objects such as satellites, and guide astronauts on space walks. Its two 11-foot arms are attached to a 12-foot body.

**Dextre is attached permanently to the side of the station.**

**In the station, astronauts control Dextre with joy sticks.**

# EXPLORING ROBOTS THAT FLY

Look, up in the sky . . . it's a robot! Unmanned aircraft may soon become a common sight in the clouds. Large or small, these flying machines are controlled by programming or by pilots on the ground. These flying bots help the military, scientists, and many other people chase enemies, make maps, watch for whales, and much more.

U.S. AIR FORCE

## Military Flyers

**48**

**51**

## Small Robot Planes

**Eyes in the Sky**

**52**

**Hovering Bots**

**55**

# FLY

Almost like a video game, the control sticks and computer terminals are used to fly the aircraft remotely.

The Global Hawk takes in air here; the jets at the back then power it skyward.

U.S. AIR FORCE

## Military Map Quester

The R4 Global Hawk soars above the desert. Its multiple cameras provide detailed images of the ground below. The Air Force then creates maps for use by ground troops.

## Flying Viking

Pilots look over the Viking unmanned aircraft before they steer it into the sky. It files over battlefields and sends back live video images.

303

A jet-like rocket blasts the drone into the sky.

## One-Way Flight

The U.S. Air Force uses unmanned aircraft like this drone to train pilots and ground troops on how to destroy enemy missiles. These kinds of training exercises keep pilots and ground troops safe.

The nose contains numerous cameras and sensors.

Unmanned aircraft are getting smaller and smaller, letting soldiers use them in more ways.

## Hand Launch

Unmanned aircraft like Raven can take on dangerous missions and save solders' lives. Instead of sending soldiers to patrol a combat zone, Raven can go and send back video surveillance. The craft acts as the military's eyes in the sky.

The Puma craft is launched by hand from a boat.

The ocean is enormous, so scientists need many ways to check it out. Putting "eyes in the sky" with unmanned aircraft is fast becoming a big part of ocean exploration.

## Up and Away!

On this speedboat near the Florida Keys, experts from the National Oceanic and Atmospheric Administration (NOAA) are launching an unmanned craft called a Puma. NOAA is using aircraft like these to help research whale and fish migration, to study ways to help clean up oil spills, and to track ocean pollution. Information the aircrafts gather will help protect the world's oceans.

A speedboat tracked the whale in the water.

## A Whale of a Photo

The Puma unmanned aircraft (shown above) took this amazing photo of a blue whale just below the surface of the Pacific Ocean. Aerial images such as these will help scientists understand and protect whales.

Blue whales can be more than 100 feet long!

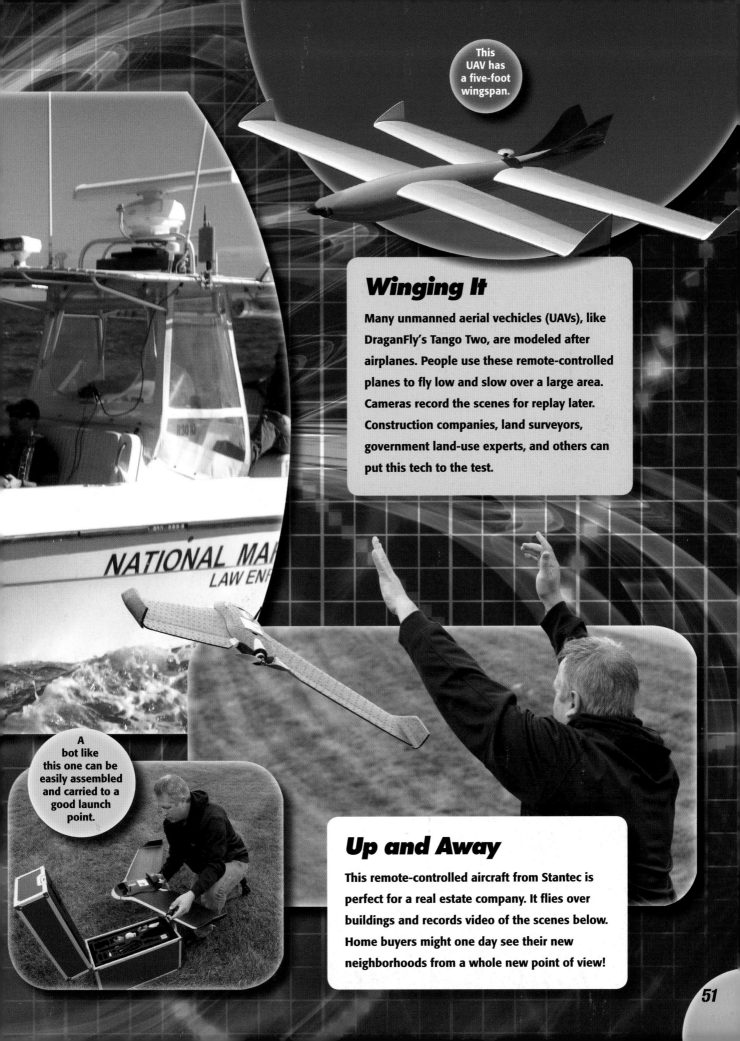

This
UAV has
a five-foot
wingspan.

## Winging It

Many unmanned aerial vechicles (UAVs), like DraganFly's Tango Two, are modeled after airplanes. People use these remote-controlled planes to fly low and slow over a large area. Cameras record the scenes for replay later. Construction companies, land surveyors, government land-use experts, and others can put this tech to the test.

A
bot like
this one can be
easily assembled
and carried to a
good launch
point.

## Up and Away

This remote-controlled aircraft from Stantec is perfect for a real estate company. It flies over buildings and records video of the scenes below. Home buyers might one day see their new neighborhoods from a whole new point of view!

**The craft can be launched by hand.**

## Eye in the Sky

This Swinglet CAM from SenseFly could be called a flying camera. The tiny aircraft snaps images that can be used to make aerial maps, or monitor wildlife, crops, and traffic.

**These tiny bots are made of low-cost plastic.**

## In the Wind

Unmanned aerial vehicles (UAVs) are helping scientists learn about hurricanes. Engineers at the University of Florida created a mini-flyer packed with tiny instruments to record wind and weather. Hundreds of these UAVs released into a hurricane or tornado might one day provide researchers a better picture of these storms.

On-board screen lets user check video upon landing.

Its wings span 31 inches and are made of sturdy foam.

This diagram shows how this bot takes video and still pictures in a grid pattern.

These are samples of images that high-flying UAVs take.

# FLY

## Popular Bots

Quadcopters such as this one have become popular among aviation-lovers young and old. The craft can zoom, swoop, and hover just like a helicopter. It can be equipped with cameras to take awesome aerial pix.

Quadcopters come in many sizes. Some are small and toy-like; many kids have these. Others are more complicated and call for more flying skill.

The quadcopter's arms twist or rotate to make the copter rise or descend.

This quad has a camera suspended from the bottom.

High-end copters come with base stations.

Here's an octo-copter (eight blades) and its remote control console.

## Hovercraft

Here's a look from below at a remote copter with six blades. It takes practice to get this craft to stand still in midair!

**The K-Max can lift almost three tons of material!**

## Chopper UAV

This helicopter can safely transport supplies to troops in combat zones. That's because there is something missing —the pilot! The K-Max helicopter is one of the few choppers that can fly unmanned. The pilot is actually on the ground operating the controls remotely.

## Tiny Flyer

The Black Hornet is only a few inches long, but it has a big job. The British Army uses these tiny UAVs as spies. The Hornet can hover over a battlefield and send back pictures. It can go where larger aircraft can't. It's hard to spot such a small intruder!

**The tiny flyer is launched right from a soldier's hand.**

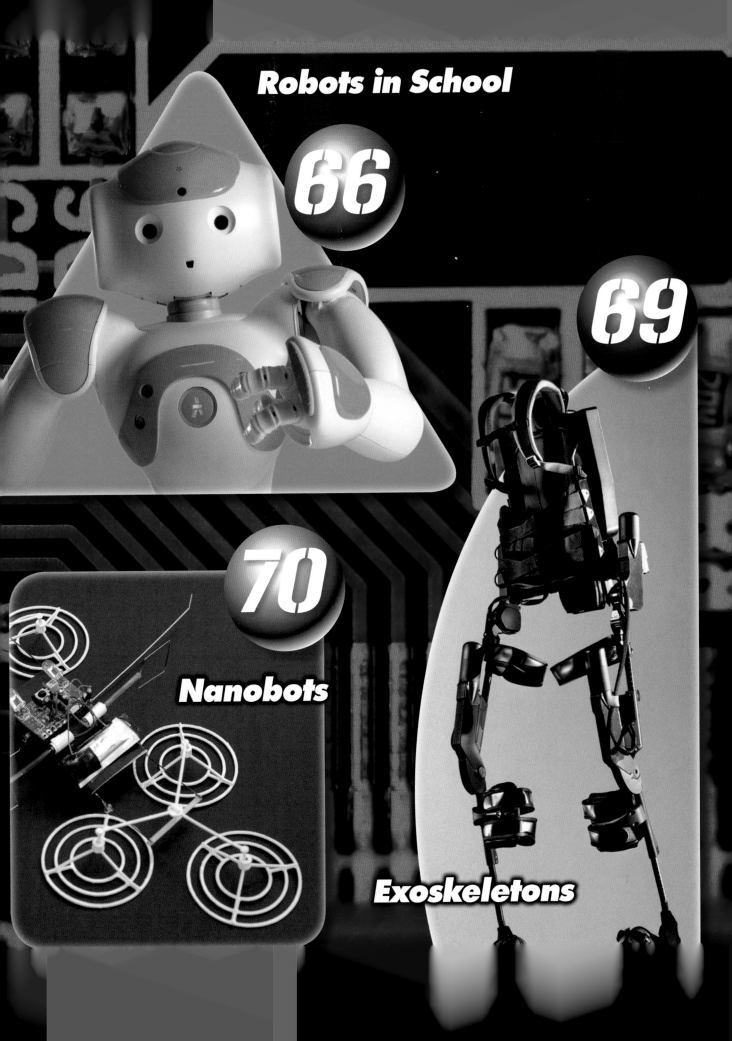

**Robots in School** 66

69

70

**Nanobots**

**Exoskeletons**

# EXPLORING ROBOTS THAT HELP

Robots are assisting doctors in the operating room. Expert surgeons use the machines shown in this photo to make operations faster, and easier on patients. Robots won't replace doctors, but they can help doctors help you.

The surgeon gets a close-up view of the operation site on a screen. He uses hand controls to move the instruments in the patient.

With two video screens, a pair of surgeons can work side-by-side. Each controls a different instrument.

## Calling Doctor Robot!

Robots allow surgeons to operate with superhuman precision. The machines shown here are part of the DaVinci Surgical System. Using this technology, surgeons always have a steady hand. They can manipulate tiny instruments, making much smaller incisions in patients than were possible before. Smaller cuts mean faster recovery time. Robots aren't cutting surgeons out of a job. They just lend a helping, steady hand.

# EXPLORING ROBOTS THAT HELP

A nurse carries a virtual doc from patient to patient.

## Doctor on the Go

Doctors visit patients via smart pads like this RP-7. The doctor can view records and answer questions.

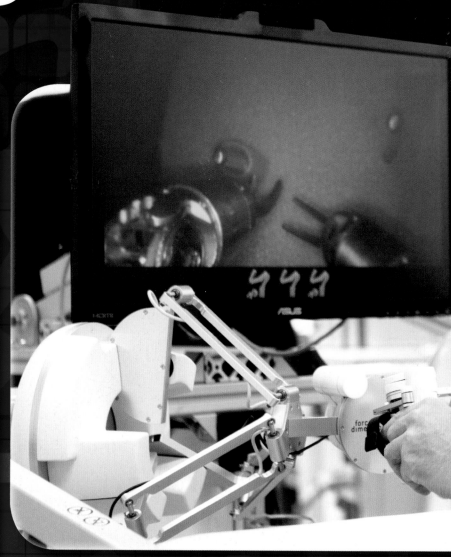

## Practice Time

Surgeons practice robotic surgery with exercises like this one. They learn to operate remote controls to move tiny instruments inside a human body.

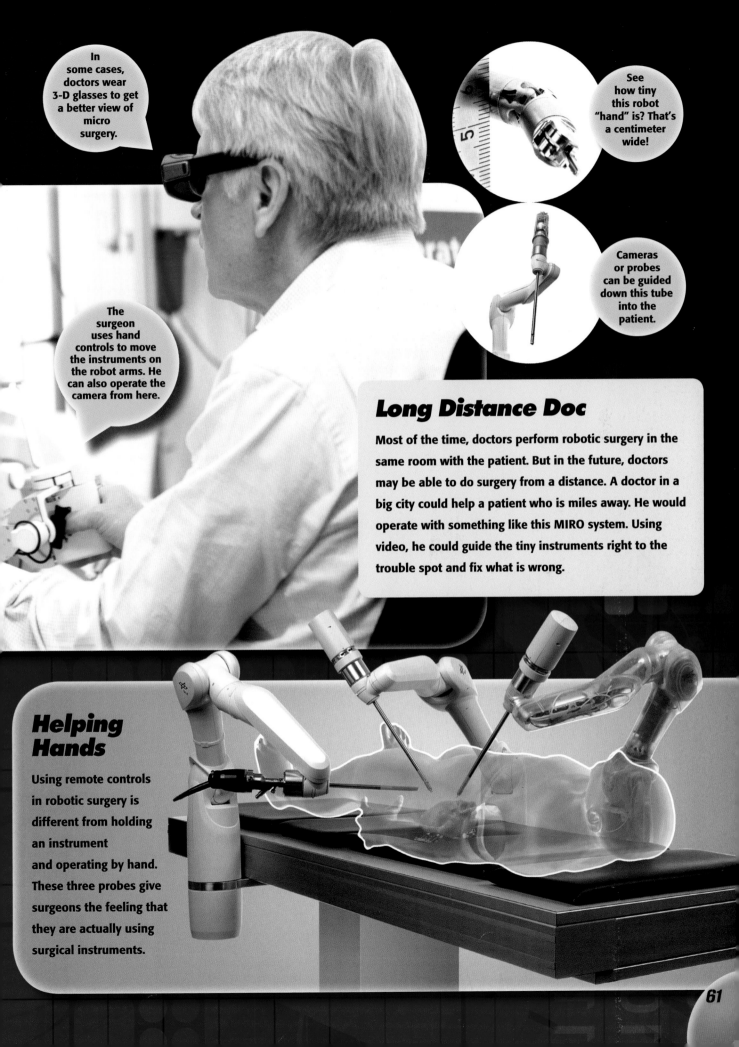

In some cases, doctors wear 3-D glasses to get a better view of micro surgery.

See how tiny this robot "hand" is? That's a centimeter wide!

Cameras or probes can be guided down this tube into the patient.

The surgeon uses hand controls to move the instruments on the robot arms. He can also operate the camera from here.

## Long Distance Doc

Most of the time, doctors perform robotic surgery in the same room with the patient. But in the future, doctors may be able to do surgery from a distance. A doctor in a big city could help a patient who is miles away. He would operate with something like this MIRO system. Using video, he could guide the tiny instruments right to the trouble spot and fix what is wrong.

## Helping Hands

Using remote controls in robotic surgery is different from holding an instrument and operating by hand. These three probes give surgeons the feeling that they are actually using surgical instruments.

# EXPLORING ROBOTS THAT HELP

Yes, cats like to ride on robot vacuum cleaners.

## Vacu-bot

This E-Ziclean is one of several types of robots that automatically vacuum floors by moving around a room on its own.

Can robots help around the house? That's one of the biggest areas of robot development: Machines that help us live our lives.

## Amazing Asimo

Asimo, made by Honda, is one of the world's most advanced robots. The humanoid bot can walk on uneven surfaces, climb stairs, hop on one leg, and even run 5.6 miles. Thirsty? Asimo can open a thermos and pour its contents into a cup! Versions of Asimo work at Honda headquarters, help at conferences, and "perform" at places such as Disneyland.

The blades spin as the robot moves forward.

Asimo's legs have the same joints as in a human leg.

Sensors in the feet help Asimo keep its balance.

## Gutter-bot

No more climbing ladders to clean gutters! Just put this Looj robot to work. It zooms through gutters, churning out leaves and other debris.

The Mahru-Z is about 4 feet tall.

Mahru-Z can work while plugged in or on a battery.

Pool cleaning bots are waterproof to protect the electronics inside.

## Robot Maid

Korean scientists created Mahru-Z, a walking humanoid robot that can be programmed to help around the house. Mahru-Z can vacuum, prepare food in a microwave, and even put clothes into a washing machine. Whether you put an apron on yours is up to you!

## Underwater Robotics

Don't feel like cleaning the swimming pool? Let a robot do the work for you. While you're relaxing poolside, the iRobot vacuums up dirt, leaves, and other debris from the bottom and sides of the pool. You can even program the machine to keep the water chemically-balanced. What can't the iRobot do? Play Marco Polo, at least not yet.

# EXPLORING ROBOTS THAT HELP

The heavy roll cage was built for safety—just in case!

## Road Robots

A blind person can drive this car! Cameras and sensors in the vehicle, built by students at Virginia Tech, tell the driver what to do. You won't see this car on the road yet, but its development is a big step forward in making cars that can "think" for themselves.

A rooftop sensor gives information to the car's computer.

## Who's Driving?

Google is road-testing cars that steer, stop, and start without a human driver. Engineers say driverless cars are safer because the computers react more quickly than humans.

Will robots drive our cars? This is one of the biggest areas of robot research. Many companies are trying to find ways to make cars smart and safe enough to drive themselves.

Sensors "read" the road ahead to look for obstacles.

The back end of the CityCar squeezes in to make parking a snap.

## Tiny Ride

Never look for a parking place again! The CityCar can change shape to fit into small spaces. All four wheels turn to move in any direction.

## Riding Robots

To test its oil products, Castrol created Flossie, a robot that rides a motorcycle. Flossie doesn't ride on a road, however. It stays in one place, but it can shift gears, work the throttle, and use the brakes. A robot can ride for much longer than a human test driver.

Flossie can ride in any weather.

## Making Tracks

A blind driver is behind the wheel of this Ford Explorer. With the help of technology developed by Virginia Tech students, the driver steered around the Daytona International Speedway in Florida.

# HELP

reach more students in the classroom. These hi-tech teaching assistants can provide students with one-on-one help in just about any subject.

## Reading Robot

Schools are using robots such as NAO to work with students. NAO has a camera and voice recorder and can be programmed to help students with reading, basic math skills, and communication. Teachers can program lessons into NAO, which can respond to student's questions and answers.

NAO robots are the perfect size for standing on desks to work with students.

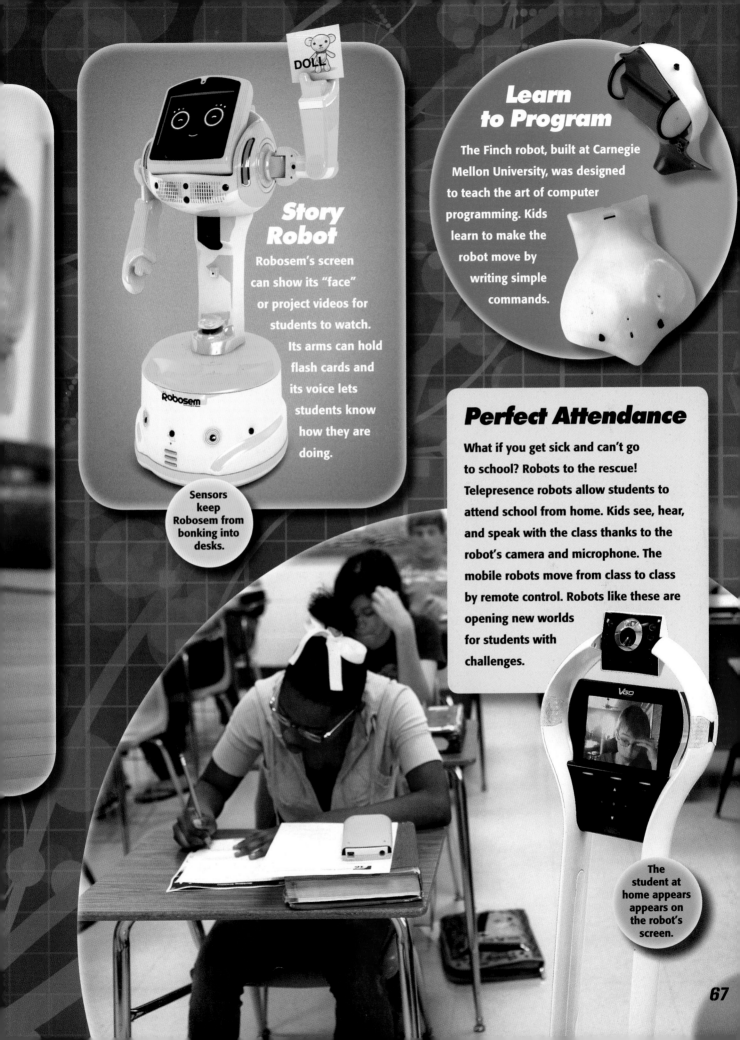

## Story Robot

Robosem's screen can show its "face" or project videos for students to watch. Its arms can hold flash cards and its voice lets students know how they are doing.

DOLL

Sensors keep Robosem from bonking into desks.

## Learn to Program

The Finch robot, built at Carnegie Mellon University, was designed to teach the art of computer programming. Kids learn to make the robot move by writing simple commands.

## Perfect Attendance

What if you get sick and can't go to school? Robots to the rescue! Telepresence robots allow students to attend school from home. Kids see, hear, and speak with the class thanks to the robot's camera and microphone. The mobile robots move from class to class by remote control. Robots like these are opening new worlds for students with challenges.

The student at home appears appears on the robot's screen.

# HELP

Insects have strong exoskeletons, or outer coverings, that protect and strengthen them. Can robot exoskeletons do the same for humans?

## Super Soldier

Soldiers wearing this XOS-2 robot suit can do the work of three people. They can lift 17 times more weight in the suit than without it. These suits could help soldiers do their jobs better and more safely.

The key to this suit is hydraulics. That is the science of using fluid to create power.

A backpack holds the battery that powers the arm.

Titan

## Power to You!

To help people with back injuries recover faster, students at the University of Pennsylvania created the Titan Arm. The device's cables and electronics aid lifting and rehabilitate muscles.

A battery pack powers the X1 suit.

The legs are strapped to the wearer.

## Space Skeleton

NASA's X-1 exoskeleton can help astronauts work longer and more effectively. The robot-powered legs help the astronaut control movements in zero gravity, while also providing more lifting power.

## Cyborg Action!

A cyborg is a mix of a human and a robot. Cyberdyne's HAL suit is one step toward a cyborg future. The suit provides strength for injured people or lifting power for workers.

## Robots for Rehab

People with severe spinal injuries are walking again, thanks to robots like Ekso. Metal braces support the legs, while a battery pack provides power. The user controls the movements with help from onboard computer systems. Robots like Ekso are changing lives!

Ekso helps this injured woman walk again!

Sensors help the user stay balanced.

# EXPLORING ROBOTS THAT HELP

It's time for tiny robots! Scientists are looking at ways to make robots so small they can't be seen even with a microscope. This is the science of nanotechnology. Who knows what nanobots might do?

Each "foot" is about the size of a paper clip, or 1.5 inches across.

These tiny wires act as oars to move the bot.

## Water Walker

The water-spider robot may someday clean up oil spills. The bot, built by scientists at Carnegie Mellon University, is so small and light, it can "walk" on water. Thousands of them could one day be unleashed into a spill zone to help clean up the mess. This is one tiny robot you can see, but others are smaller than the period at the end of this sentence.

The entire mini-robot is only 4 inches across.

# The Buzz About RoboBees

Scientists at Harvard University created RoboBees in the hope that these tiny robots could help with the work of real bees. Each RoboBee has a tiny clamp at the bottom that could carry pollen or seeds directly to fields and flowers.

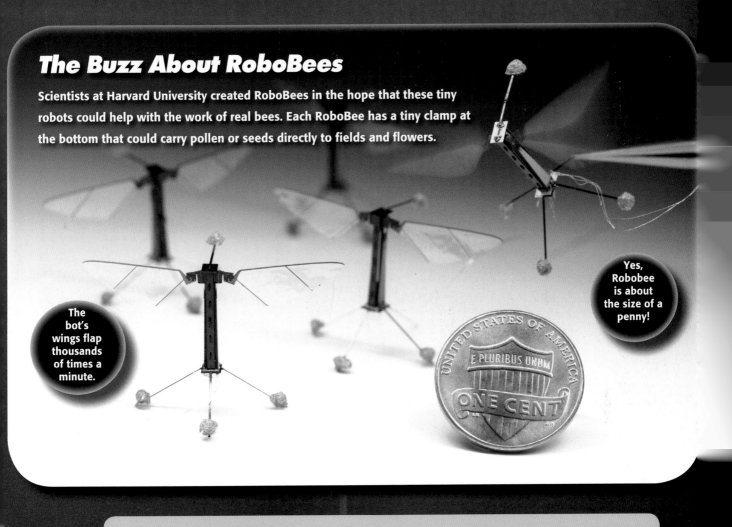

The bot's wings flap thousands of times a minute.

Yes, Robobee is about the size of a penny!

UNITED STATES OF AMERICA
E PLURIBUS UNUM
ONE CENT

# Come Together

This cube is actually a tiny robot that can move independently. Hundreds of these cube-shaped robots could snap together to form a chair, table, ladder or other object on command.

Compare the box bot to this gold ring for size.

Each box bot is packed with electronics and sensors.

# EXPLORING ROBOTS THAT PLAY

All play and no work sounds pretty good, especially when a robot's involved. It's not the future . . . it's happening now. Robots are battling, but they never get hurt. Robots play soccer and shoot hoops, hardly ever missing a shot. Kids can even own a robot pet that comes when they call. And it won't leave a mess!

**Old-Time Toy**

**75**

**Smartphone Bot**

**74**

**80**

**Soccer Robots**

# PLAY

## Mobile Helper

The Hovis Genie takes its instructions from an Android phone, and once it's moving, it's a do-everything robot! It can spin in a full circle, take pictures and video, record messages and play them back, act as a mobile alarm clock, and much more. Here is one of its coolest features: Let's say you're at a friend's house and need to remind your sister to feed the cat. Call the Genie, and it will find your sister and deliver the message. You can't put a price on excellent service.

A dock on the chest holds the smart phone that is giving the order.

## Dancebot

The RoboSapien can perform high-tech moves. You can program it to do different dances.

A sensor inside the Genie detects objects in its path.

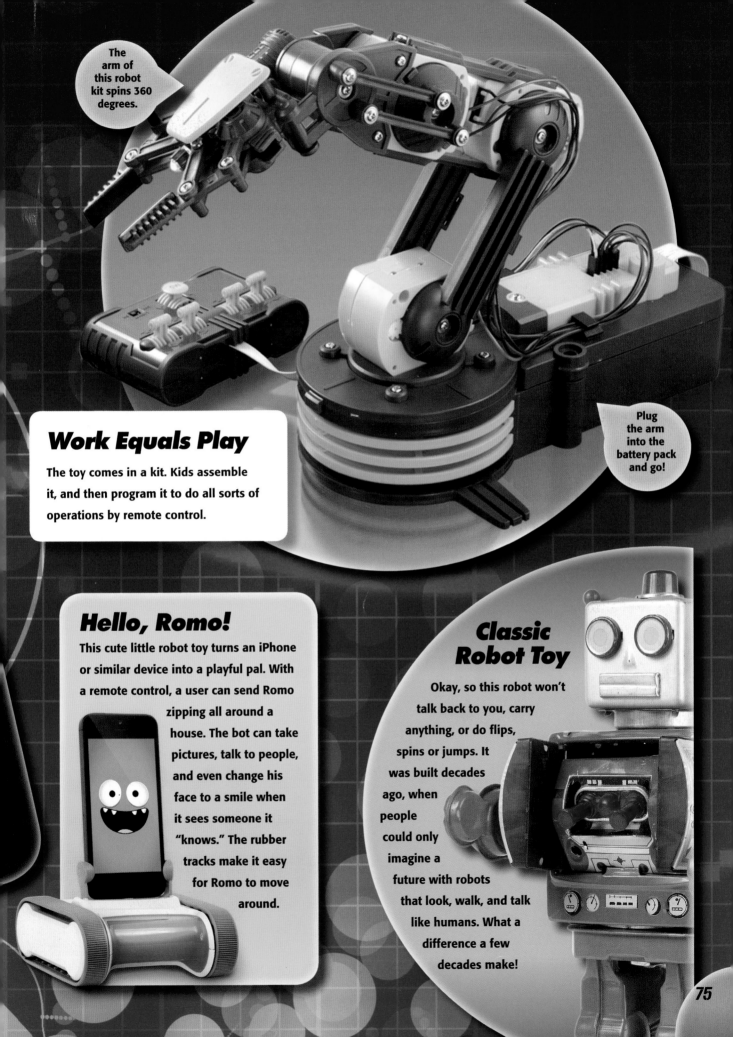

The arm of this robot kit spins 360 degrees.

## Work Equals Play

The toy comes in a kit. Kids assemble it, and then program it to do all sorts of operations by remote control.

Plug the arm into the battery pack and go!

## Hello, Romo!

This cute little robot toy turns an iPhone or similar device into a playful pal. With a remote control, a user can send Romo zipping all around a house. The bot can take pictures, talk to people, and even change his face to a smile when it sees someone it "knows." The rubber tracks make it easy for Romo to move around.

## Classic Robot Toy

Okay, so this robot won't talk back to you, carry anything, or do flips, spins or jumps. It was built decades ago, when people could only imagine a future with robots that look, walk, and talk like humans. What a difference a few decades make!

# PLAY

Toy robots are more than just play things. They can teach kids the basics of programming, which is tech-speak for telling the bot what to do. Now that's playing it smart.

## You're in Control

Yana (left) and Bo are toy robots that kids can program. Using a tablet or smartphone, kids can send instructions to the two robots to make them move, roll, play, or perform.

## Here, Robot!

Genibo is one of several robot dogs. This toy robot responds to many commands like "Roll over!" and "Sit!"

Nose-cam? Genibo has a camera in its nose!

Kids can get connectors to let Bo and Yana "play" together.

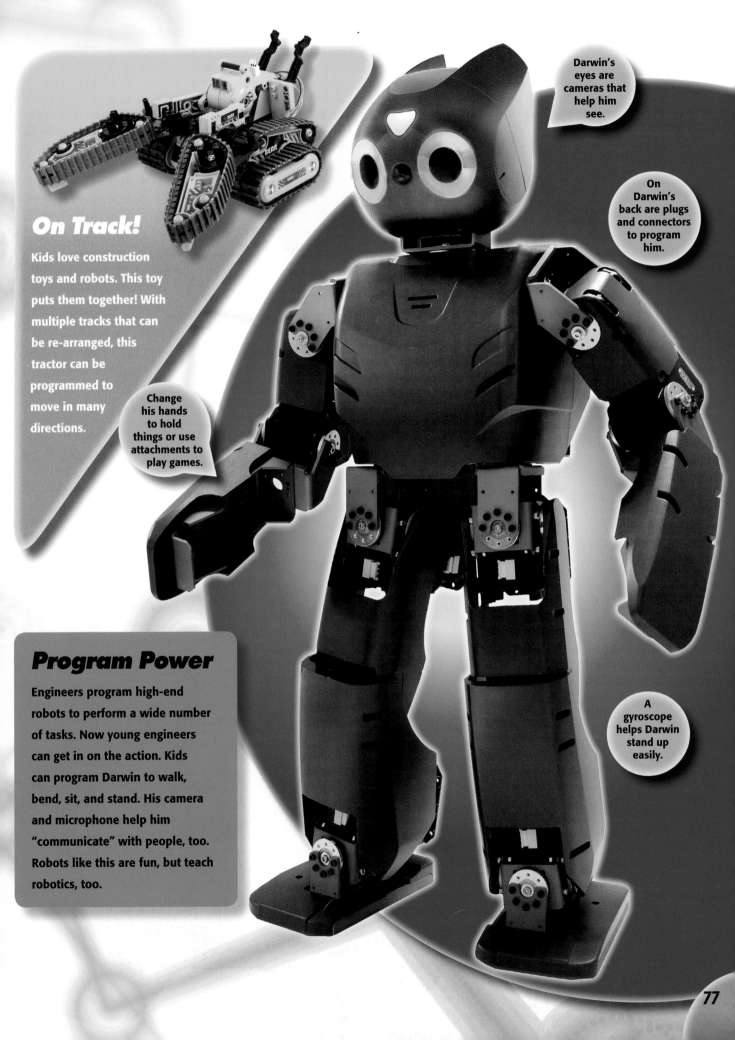

## On Track!

Kids love construction toys and robots. This toy puts them together! With multiple tracks that can be re-arranged, this tractor can be programmed to move in many directions.

Darwin's eyes are cameras that help him see.

On Darwin's back are plugs and connectors to program him.

Change his hands to hold things or use attachments to play games.

## Program Power

Engineers program high-end robots to perform a wide number of tasks. Now young engineers can get in on the action. Kids can program Darwin to walk, bend, sit, and stand. His camera and microphone help him "communicate" with people, too. Robots like this are fun, but teach robotics, too.

A gyroscope helps Darwin stand up easily.

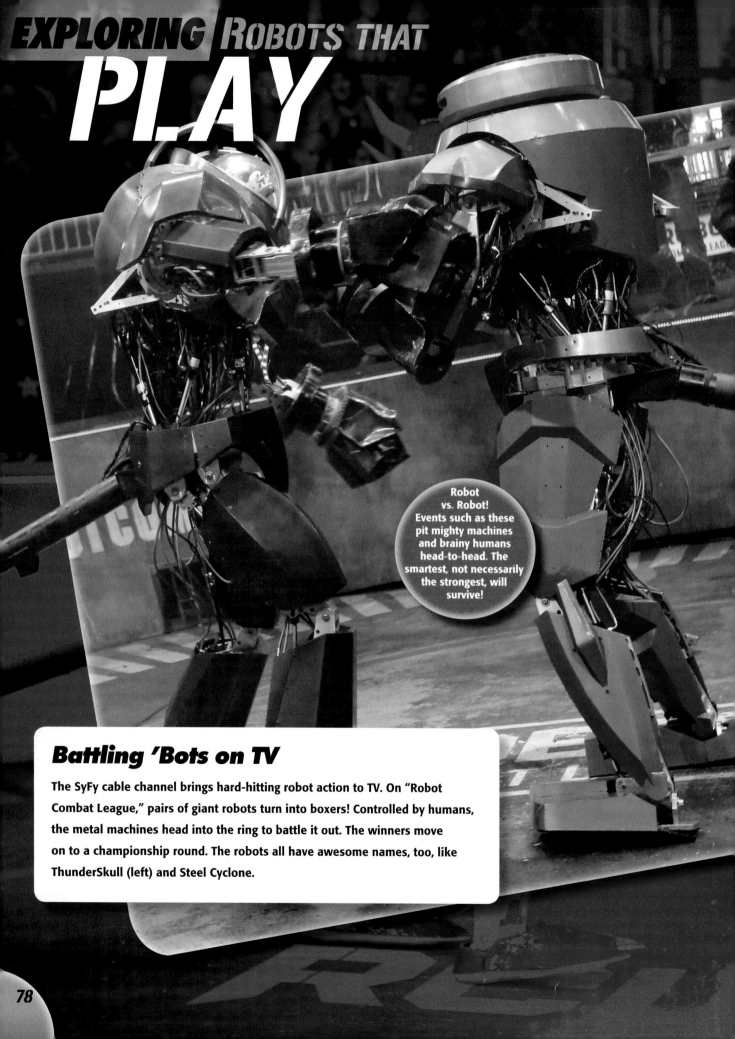

# EXPLORING ROBOTS THAT PLAY

Robot vs. Robot! Events such as these pit mighty machines and brainy humans head-to-head. The smartest, not necessarily the strongest, will survive!

## Battling 'Bots on TV

The SyFy cable channel brings hard-hitting robot action to TV. On "Robot Combat League," pairs of giant robots turn into boxers! Controlled by humans, the metal machines head into the ring to battle it out. The winners move on to a championship round. The robots all have awesome names, too, like ThunderSkull (left) and Steel Cyclone.

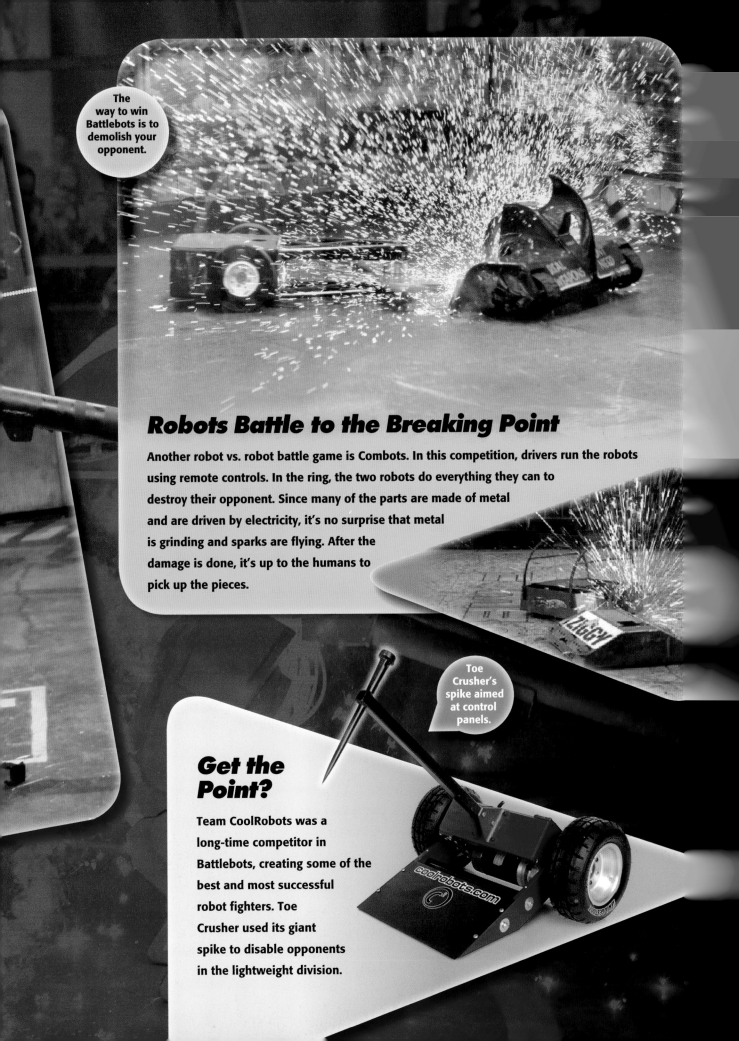

**The way to win Battlebots is to demolish your opponent.**

# Robots Battle to the Breaking Point

Another robot vs. robot battle game is Combots. In this competition, drivers run the robots using remote controls. In the ring, the two robots do everything they can to destroy their opponent. Since many of the parts are made of metal and are driven by electricity, it's no surprise that metal is grinding and sparks are flying. After the damage is done, it's up to the humans to pick up the pieces.

**Toe Crusher's spike aimed at control panels.**

## Get the Point?

Team CoolRobots was a long-time competitor in Battlebots, creating some of the best and most successful robot fighters. Toe Crusher used its giant spike to disable opponents in the lightweight division.

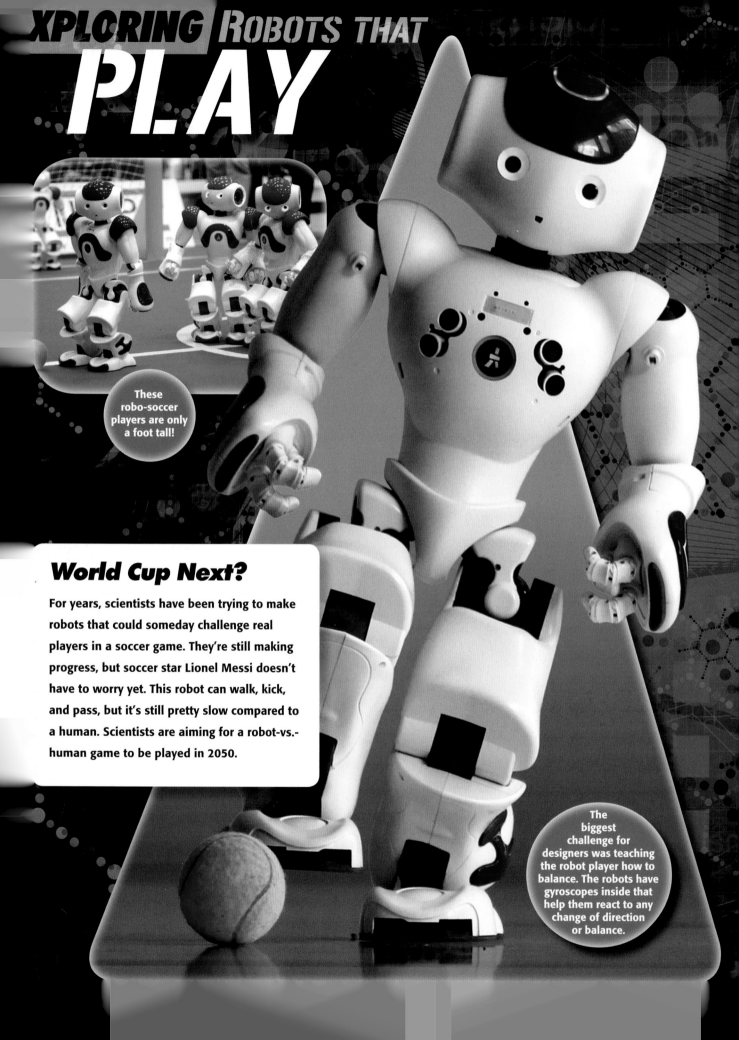

# XPLORING ROBOTS THAT PLAY

These robo-soccer players are only a foot tall!

## World Cup Next?

For years, scientists have been trying to make robots that could someday challenge real players in a soccer game. They're still making progress, but soccer star Lionel Messi doesn't have to worry yet. This robot can walk, kick, and pass, but it's still pretty slow compared to a human. Scientists are aiming for a robot-vs.-human game to be played in 2050.

The biggest challenge for designers was teaching the robot player how to balance. The robots have gyroscopes inside that help them react to any change of direction or balance.

# Robot Jockeys!

Yes, those are robots on the back of camels. In Saudi Arabia, camel racers are experimenting with robot jockeys.

# Infinite Hoop

In 2012, the FIRST Robotics competition challenged teams to make a robot that would shoot baskets. Robots used light sensors to aim and then toss balls toward the hoop. They almost never missed!

Reflective tape on the baskets helped the robots aim.

# RoboPong

Imagine playing ping-pong against an opponent that never gets tired! Scientists at Zhejiang University in China created this robot and to test its reflexes, showed it how to play ping-pong. The bot uses high-speed cameras to track the ball and super-fast processors to move its arm to return a shot.

This is Wu, one of a pair of ping-pong-playing robots.

# KIDS MAKE

You—yes, you!—can make a robot today. Kids everywhere are doing incredible things with make-it-yourself robots. Just follow the steps to build your own creation. Want to go even further? Join a team and compete against other students. You'll be amazed at the incredible things you can program your new robot to do. Get going!

**84**

## LEGO Mindstorms

**85**

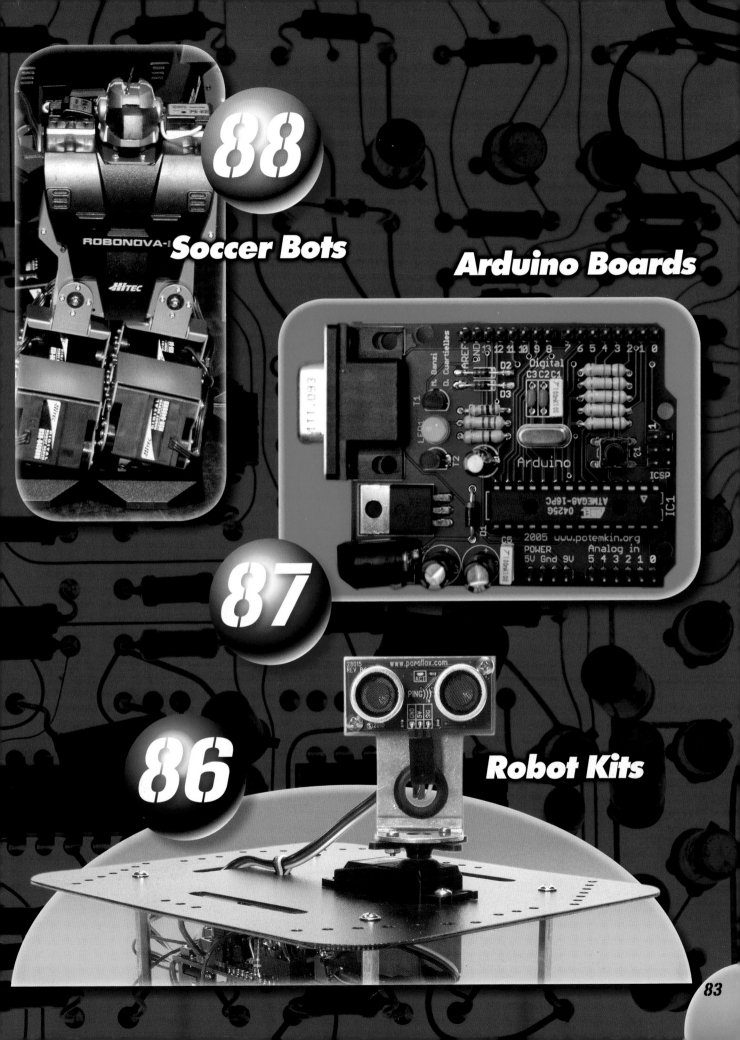

**88**

**Soccer Bots**

**Arduino Boards**

**87**

**86**

**Robot Kits**

# EXPLORING ROBOTS THAT
# KIDS MAKE

## Mindstorms

This LEGO Mindstorms robot, called Everstorm, can roll on tracks, fire missiles, and move its arms on command.

Kids can now become robot makers themselves. LEGO Mindstorms are powered by a tiny processor built into a LEGO brick. The rest takes the power of imagination.

A rack on the arm holds plastic balls that Everstorm shoots.

Your instructions for the robot are sent by Bluetooth or USB.

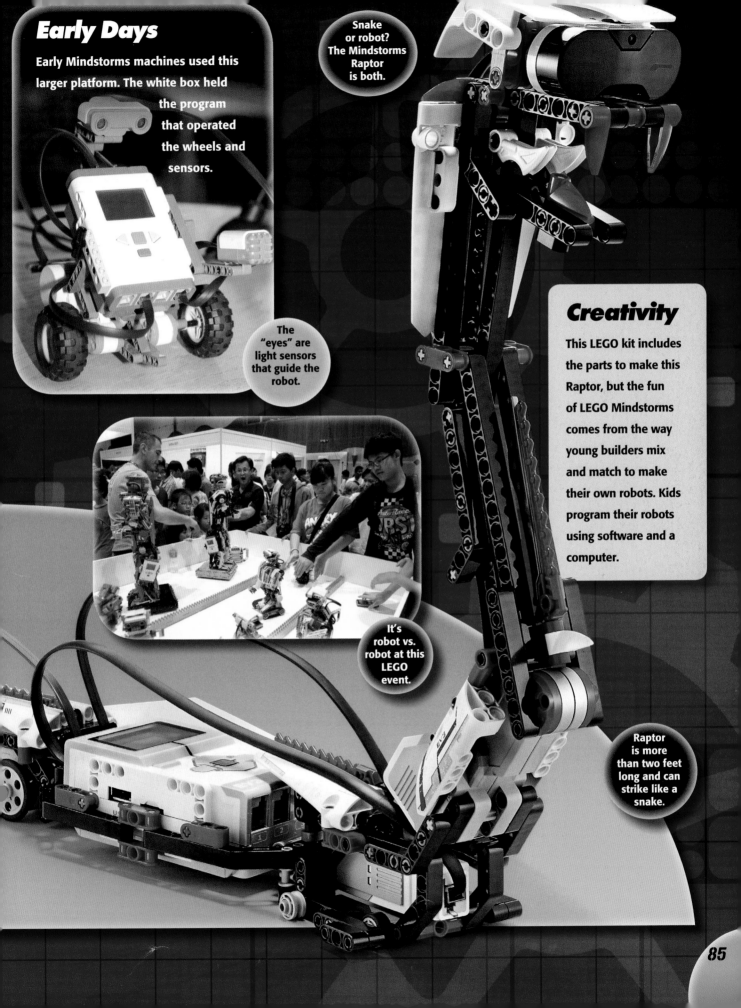

# Early Days

Early Mindstorms machines used this larger platform. The white box held the program that operated the wheels and sensors.

Snake or robot? The Mindstorms Raptor is both.

The "eyes" are light sensors that guide the robot.

It's robot vs. robot at this LEGO event.

# Creativity

This LEGO kit includes the parts to make this Raptor, but the fun of LEGO Mindstorms comes from the way young builders mix and match to make their own robots. Kids program their robots using software and a computer.

Raptor is more than two feet long and can strike like a snake.

# EXPLORING ROBOTS THAT KIDS MAKE

## Rovera 4WD

This robot starts as a box of parts. Kids transform the pieces into a rolling machine that can sense its surroundings. Builders learn how to use circuit boards to send electronic signals to the machine to make it work.

LEGO is not the only way to make robots. Many companies sell robot kits. Those include all the parts to make a robot, but it's left to the kids to build and wire them for action.

## Just Get to Work

Here's an example of what a robot kit looks like before it becomes a robot. It looks complicated, but follow the directions and you'll do just fine.

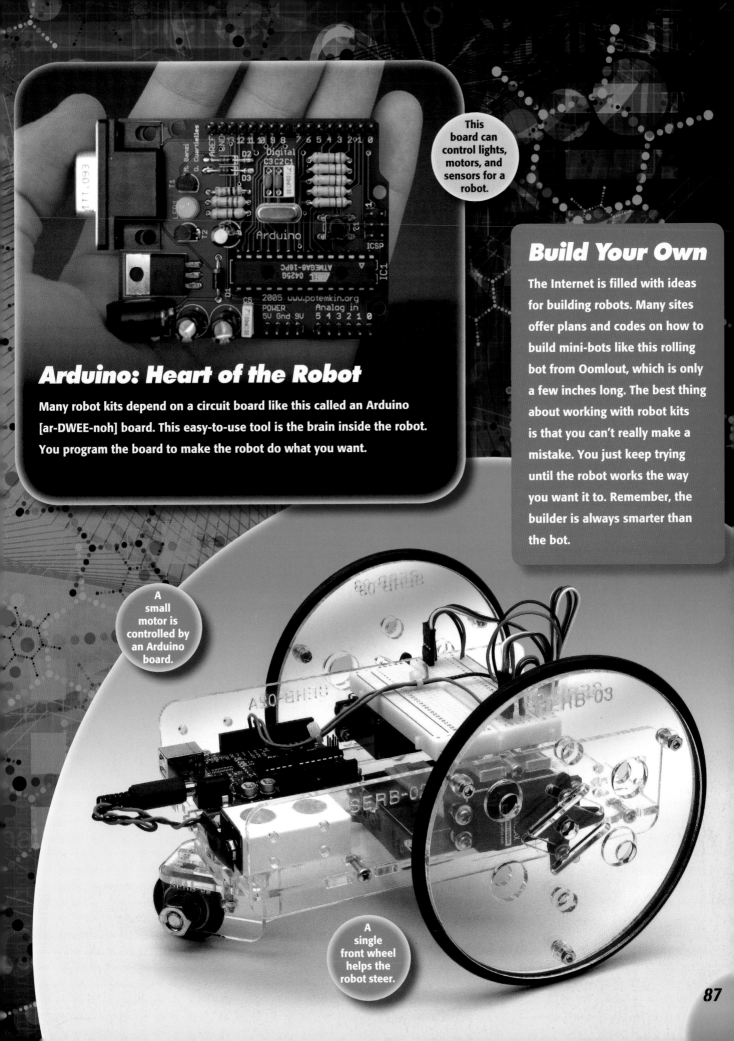

## Arduino: Heart of the Robot

Many robot kits depend on a circuit board like this called an Arduino [ar-DWEE-noh] board. This easy-to-use tool is the brain inside the robot. You program the board to make the robot do what you want.

> This board can control lights, motors, and sensors for a robot.

## Build Your Own

The Internet is filled with ideas for building robots. Many sites offer plans and codes on how to build mini-bots like this rolling bot from Oomlout, which is only a few inches long. The best thing about working with robot kits is that you can't really make a mistake. You just keep trying until the robot works the way you want it to. Remember, the builder is always smarter than the bot.

> A small motor is controlled by an Arduino board.

> A single front wheel helps the robot steer.

# EXPLORING ROBOTS THAT KIDS MAKE

For some kids, robots are more than just toys or fun—they are competition! Dozens of different events around the world offer kids a chance to pit their robotic skills against each other.

## Gold Medal!

This soccer-playing robot team from the United States won the gold medal at the RoboGames. These robots, only about a foot tall, were operated by a combination of remote control and pre-programming.

## Make It Work

At robot contests, the competitors spend a lot of time working with their computers to pass along the instructions to their "athletes." This girl is programming her robot to play soccer.

**Robots in FIRST Lego League are built to perform a specific task.**

## Getting Started

Elementary school students take part in FIRST Lego League competitions. They compete to see how the robots they have built will perform against other students' robots.

**FIRST: For Inspiration and Recognition of Science and Technology.**

## Winners!

FIRST Robotics is the largest international student robot competition. Teams from schools around the world build robots to take part in games created annually by FIRST.

**FIRST Robotics Competition**

**FRC.**
FIRST®Robotics Competition

**WINNER**

**2013 LOS ANGELES REGIONAL**

1717

1717

**This team from Dos Pueblos Engineering Academy in California made a robot that threw flying discs.**

## Space Monkey?

NASA's RoboSimian is designed to be able to work upside-down as well as right-side-up. Gripper claws and rotating joints make it super-flexible.

Each year, the best robot makers in the world compete at the DARPA Challenge. This contest is run by the U.S. Defense Department. Humanoid robots are given a series of tasks, such as lifting objects, opening doors, or climbing walls. The robots that best meet the challenges become models for future robots.

## Handy Bot

Carnegie Mellon's CHIMP robot was among the best at a recent DARPA challenge. Like a human, CHIMP has thumbs that can help it grasp objects. It moves on tracks instead of legs for greater balance. Someday, CHIMP might help rescue victims of disasters.

## Walking Tall

Team Kaist from Korea sent this bot to a recent DARPA event. It did well in the walking tests, but not so well in wall-climbing. Back to the drawing board!

The head of this bot spins 360 degrees as it captures video.

## Astrobot!

NASA scientists are regular participants in the DARPA challenge. Recently, they sent Valkyrie, a humanoid robot designed to one day work in space. Teams of experts each built one part of Valkyrie before coming together to create the final product, which can make 44 different motions.

Valkyrie has a hard plastic shell over a metal "skeleton."

# FUTURE

Over a century, robots have ranged from life-sized to microscopic. What does the future hold? How will robots help us in 100 years? And will you be the one who helps find out?

Will they have lasers to blast cancer cells?

## Nano Attack

Nanotechnology is the fast-growing future of robotics. Scientists hope that tiny robots can be put inside people and given jobs that can't be done with surgery. This artist's rendering imagines a nanobot attacking cancer cells.

## Round and Round

Robots that look like humans are common. But have you ever seen a robotic snake? The Hydra robot from RoMeLa at the University of Virginia is part of a trend to create robots that can move like other animals.

Will Hydra be able to climb UP a pole?

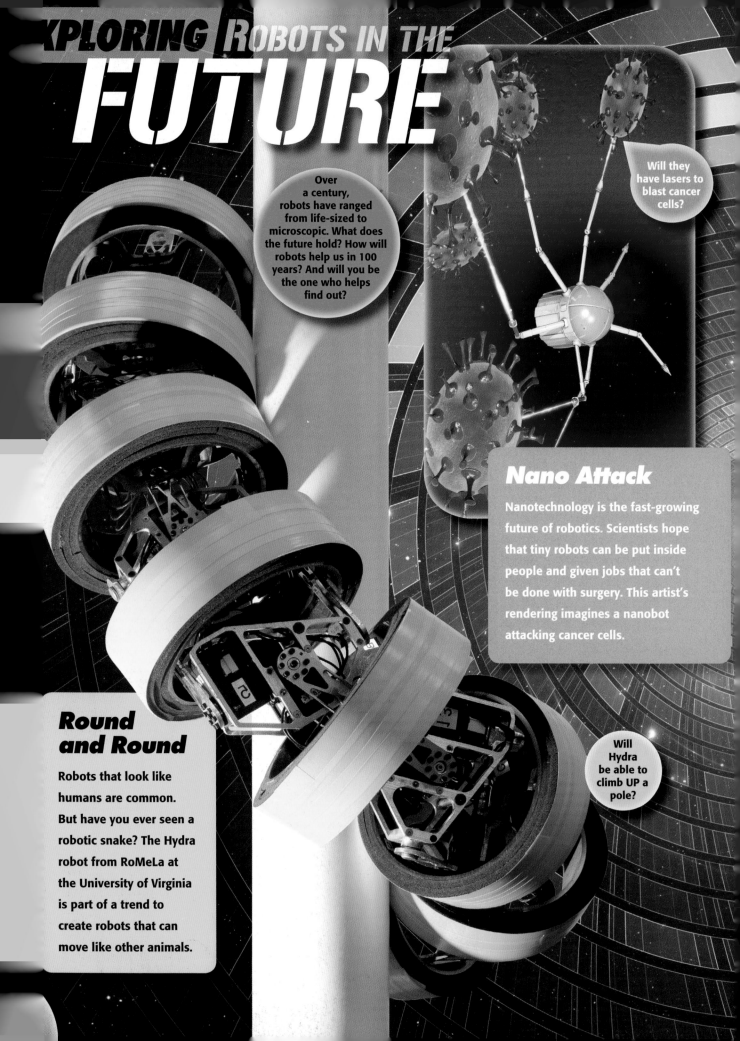

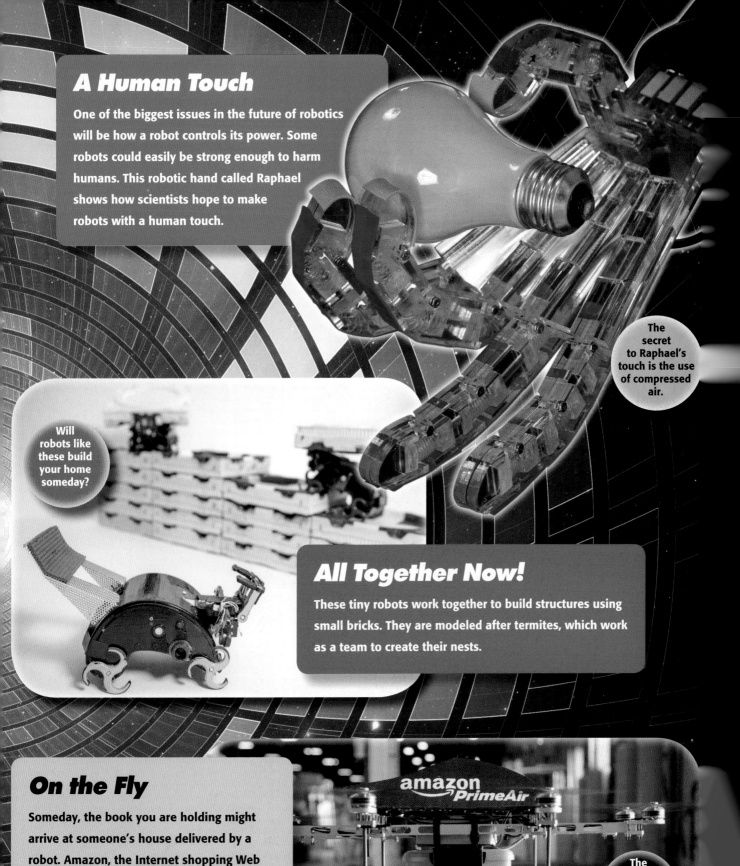

## A Human Touch

One of the biggest issues in the future of robotics will be how a robot controls its power. Some robots could easily be strong enough to harm humans. This robotic hand called Raphael shows how scientists hope to make robots with a human touch.

The secret to Raphael's touch is the use of compressed air.

Will robots like these build your home someday?

## All Together Now!

These tiny robots work together to build structures using small bricks. They are modeled after termites, which work as a team to create their nests.

## On the Fly

Someday, the book you are holding might arrive at someone's house delivered by a robot. Amazon, the Internet shopping Web site, said it is developing flying robotic drones that will deliver anything people order. Look out for incoming packages!

The drones will fly low to avoid planes.

amazon PrimeAir

# ROBOT RESOURCES

**Here are some books and Web sites that you can check out to find more information about robots of all sorts.**

## Books

**Robotics: Discover the Science and Technology of the Future with 20 Projects**
By Kathy Ceceri (Nomad Press, 2012)
This is a hands-on guide to making simple robots, often using materials you can find in your home.

**Robots** (four-book series)
By Kathryn Clay (Capstone/Blazers, 2014)
Each book in this introductory series focuses on a class of robots: helpers, factory, military, and more.

**MAKE: Lego and Arduino Projects**
By John Baichtal, Matthew Beckler, and Adam Wolf (Maker Media, 2013)
Learn all the steps to make a rolling robot, a remote-controlled light, even an automatic chocolate milk maker. The authors are part of the "maker" movement that is encouraging hands-on creative technology.

**Robotics** (series)
By Theresa Shea (Rosen, 2012)
The books in this series include titles on careers in robotics, ideas on how to build your own bot, and a robot history book.

## Apps

**Toca Robot Lab**
Build a virtual robot on your iPad from random pieces of scrap and then teach it to move.

**Make a Robot**
An Android app that lets you choose parts from a menu to create your own robot.

## Web Sites

**spaceplace.nasa.gov/muses2**
Sponsored by NASA, this site has activites for young scientists, including how to build a nanobot-like "rover."

**www.computerhistory.org**
See online exhibits and read more about how computers, robots, and the Internet evolved . . . and are still growing!

**www.firstlegoleague.org**
Find out how your school can take part in this awesome robot-building competition. The site lists contacts for parents and teachers to use to help kids sign up. Other links send robot makers to ideas pages.

**www.sciencekids.co.nz/robots.html**
This site is based in New Zealand, and it's packed with robot facts, quizzes, trivia, and projects.

Plus, ask your parents or teachers to look around your town or area for robotics classes or clubs. Many museums and science centers offer hands-on robot-building events, too. Stores sell kits that can help you learn the basics of robotics.

*Note to Parents and Teachers: These Web sites were open at the time of publication. As with anything on the Web, they are subject to change. Kids should always be guided in the best and safest practices for Web surfing.*

# PHOTO CREDITS

t: top; b: bottom; r: right; l: left; c: center

Cover Credits:
Front: NASA/DARPA (main); NASA/JPL (top); Honda Corp. (center);Florida International University Discovery Lab (bottom).
Back: DARPA (main); US Air Force (top); Dreamstime.com/Theowl84 (center); Maker Co. (bottom).

Interior: Aldeberan: 66 (2); Amazon: 93b; Boston Dynamics: 30, 31b (2), 32tl; Bristol Robotics Lab and Ian Horsfield—Alan Winfield photo 11b; Buffalo Historical Society: 10t; Canadian Space Agency: 44r (3), 45; Carnegie Mellon/Ken Andreyo: 9t, 67tr, 70; Castrol: 65cr; Combots: 79t; Corbis: 13cl; Cyberdyne: 69t; DARPA/Boston Dynamics: 33(2); DLR/Miro: 60-61 (5); Dongbu Robot: 76bl (2); Dos Pueblos Engineering Academy: 89b; Dragan Flyer: 8l, 51tr; Dreamstime.com: A1stock 3, Viorel Dudau 9b, Beercates 12c, Marek Redusiuk 15b, Buurserstraat386 54c, Andreas Weiss 74bl, Typhoonski, 81tl, Andreus 93c, 85t, 85c; Ekso Bionics: 69br (2); E-Ziclean: 62t; FIRST Robotics: 6, 81r, 89t; Florida International University/Discovery Lab: 27r; Genibo: 15t; Getty Images News/Sean Gallup: 23b; AFP 63t; Getty Image/Hulton Archive: 12t; Getty Images/Science & Picture Library: 12bl; Getty Images/Time & Life Picture Collection/Ralph Crane: 13b; Getty Images/CBS Photo Archive: 14c; Greg Goebel: 11r; Google: 64bl; Getty Images/Sports Illustrated Classic/Deanne Fitzmaurice: 67b; Great White Snark: 79cr; Harvard University/Kevin Ma and Pakpong Chirarattananon: 71t; Honda: 15tr; Robert Hextall/Wikimedia: 65tr; Hovis: 74l; ICPA via Wikimedia: 18-19; InTouch Health: 60l; Intuitive Surgical Systems, Inc./2014: 58-59; iRobot: 32tr, 32bl, 63b(2); iStock.com/canacat: 92t; Johns Hopkins University/Applied Physics Laboratory. For permission to use, modify or reproduce, contact the Office of Technology Transfer at JHU/APL: 27l (4); Kaman Aerospace Group: 55t; LEGO/Mindstorms: 84l, 85r; Looj: 62b; OWI Inc: 75t, 77t; Maker: 86t; Mary Evans Picture Library: 11t; MIT: 71br; NBC Universal: 78; NASA: 14t, 40-41 (4), 44t, 69tl; NASA/DARPA: 90-91 (5); NASA/JPL: 9c; NOAA: 50 (2); Oomlout: 87b; Pal-Robotics: 6, 22, 95; Penn State: 29tl; Photos.com: 75br; Play-i: 76t (2); PowerHawk: 34b(2); Prox Dynamics: 55br (2); Raytheon: 68t; Recon Robotics: 26 (2); Reuters: David Moir 80r, Leonard Foeger 80tl; Rethink Robotics: 20, 21t (2); RoboGames/Sam Consiglio: 88t; RoboCup 2010: 88b; Robotis: 77r; Romo: 75bl; RoMeLa/Virginia Tech/Dennis Hong: 15bl, 28 (2), 29tr, 64t, 65br, 92l, 93tr; Scout: 39b; SenseFly: 53 (all); Shutterstock: Risteski Goche 8bl, Wellphoto 21b, Dmitry Kalinovsky 23t, Stephane Bidouze 55tl, Inc. 54t, Tyler Olson 54b, catwalker 62l, Chen WS 85c, Rikephotos 85t; Stantec: 51br (2);  Stanford University/InfoLab/by Nuriya Janss/artifact courtesy Victor Scheinman and Stanford CSD Robotics: 13tr; Stone Aerospace/NASA: 39t; Tecnalia.com: 18bl; Toecrusher: 79br; Tohoku University: 35b; U.S. Air Force: Senior Airman Nadine Y. Barclay 48t, Master Sgt. Mark Fortin 49tl, Bobbi Zapka 48c, Bruce Hoffman 49tr, Ann Patton 48bl, Sgt. Michael Gullory 49br, University of Florida: 52b; University of Michigan: 31tr; Virginia Tech/Amanda Loman: 38 (3); Vecna: 31tl, 35tr; Versatrax: 34t; VGo: 8r; VGTV: 29b (2); Waseda University: 13r; Woods Hole Oceanographic Institute: 39c; Xinhua: 81bl; Yujin Robot: 67tl; Nicholas Zambetti/WikiMedia: 87t.

Backgrounds: Dreamstime.com: PixelParticle 6; Kheng Ho Toh 8, 10, 12, 14, 20, 22 26, 32, 34, 38 ,40, 44, 48, 50, 52, 54, 60, 62, 66, 68, 74, 76, 84, 88; Pzaxe 16; Aleksandar Vidonevic 64; Cobalt88 24, 94; Natis76 36; Irina Zavodchikova 46; Helen Sergeyeva 56; Arcross 82; Davinci 72. Shutterstock: Wongwean 28, 30, 80, 86.

*Thanks to the many companies, universities, government agencies, and photographers who were so helpful in providing images for this book. Every effort was made to properly credit each image, but if there are any questions, please contact the publishers and any necessary corrections will be made in future editions.*

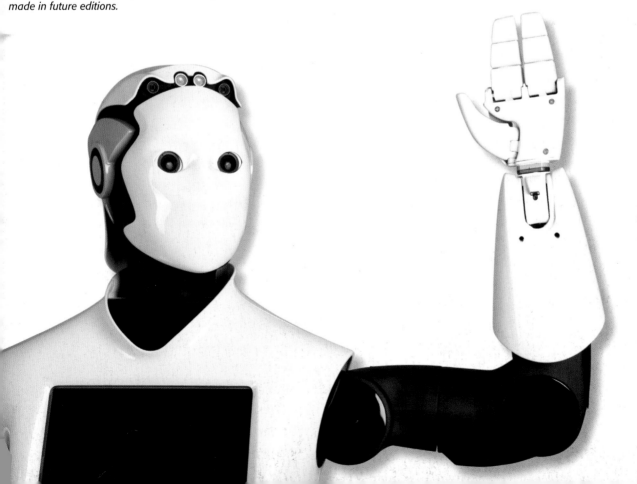

# INDEX